123

FAUVISM

FAUVISM

Joseph-Emile Muller

Thames and Hudson · London

Translated from the French by Shirley E. Jones

Contents

1 **The Formation of Fauvism**   9

2 **The Fauve Painters**   21

    Henri Matisse   23

    Maurice de Vlaminck   57

    André Derain   73

    Albert Marquet   92

    Charles Camoin, Henri Manguin, Maurice Marinot,
    Jean Puy, Louis Valtat   108

    Raoul Dufy   114

    Emile-Othon Friesz   126

    Georges Braque   130

    Kees van Dongen   137

3 **The contribution of Fauvism**   147

4 **The Dissolution of the Movement**   155

5 **Influence and Parallel Trends**   163

6 **The Survival of Fauvism**   203

7 **Conclusion**   219

8 **Biographies**   221

List of the Plates   249

Index   257

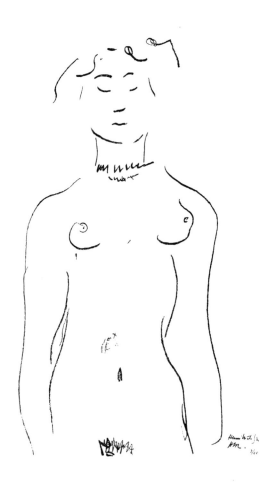

The Formation of Fauvism

Sometimes very little is needed, not for an artistic movement to be born, but for it to get its name. We speak of 'fauvism' today simply because at the Salon d'Automne in Paris in 1905 the art critic Louis Vauxcelles was struck by the effect created by a *Torso of a Child* by the sculptor Albert Marque which stood in the centre of a room filled with paintings by Matisse, Derain, Vlaminck, Friesz, Manguin, Valtat, Jean Puy and others. The torso was treated in the manner of the great Florentine sculptors, while most of the paintings were a riot of primary colours. 'The purity of this bust,' wrote Vauxcelles in *Gil Blas* (17 October 1905), 'comes as a surprise in the midst of the orgy of pure colours: it is Donatello among the wild beasts *(Donatello chez les fauves)*.' And so the word 'fauve' found its way into the vocabulary of criticism and into the history of art.

Thus there is nothing scientific about the term 'fauvism', but use has charged it with meaning and it now defines one of the most important artistic movements of the twentieth century. The importance is due to two things: first to the quality of the works, the number of exhilarating canvases given us by the fauves, and secondly to their influence, which can be seen in the works of numerous contemporary painters. However, the movement was short-lived, and it never achieved the cohesion of the impressionist or *nabi* movements. Its leaders knew each other, and some of them were friends; but they did not form what one might call a school.

The first encounters between future fauves probably took place in 1892. It was in that year that Matisse and Marquet met at evening classes at the Ecole des Arts Décoratifs in Paris and formed a friendship which was to last throughout their lives. Continuing their studies at the Ecole des Beaux-Arts, they met again in Gustave Moreau's studio, which Matisse entered in 1895 and Marquet in 1898. In fact Moreau's studio played a role in the history of fauvism which deserves special mention. Not only did it house two other painters who belonged to the movement, Camoin and Manguin, but it was also run by a very liberal teacher who encouraged his pupils to daring innovation. Moreau's painting was in itself literary and traditionalist and was hardly apt to hold their interest: the most his pupils could do was to admire his watercolours for the freedom of their patches of colour. But the master's teaching was in sharp contrast with that found in the other studios of the Ecole des Beaux-Arts, in Bonnat's or Gérôme's. 'Nature itself is of little importance,' Moreau used to say. 'It is merely a pretext for artistic expression. Art is the relentless pursuit of the expression of inward feeling by means of simple plasticity.' So it is not surprising that all his life Matisse should have spoken of his teacher with gratitude. 'He at least', he told Jacques Guenne, 'was capable of enthusiasms. One day, he would reiterate his admiration for Raphael, the next, for Veronese. Another morning he would come in and say that Chardin was the greatest master of them all. Moreau was able to pick out and show us the greatest painters, whilst Bouguereau exhorted us to admire Giulio Romano.' And to Pierre Courthion Matisse said: 'Moreau gave us no fixed line to follow. His teaching troubled us profoundly. With him, one was able to discover the sort of work most suited to one's temperament. In the minds of the young he created desires which, it must be admitted, were not always suited to their capabilities.'

After Moreau's death in 1898, Matisse was asked by the new professor, Cormon, to leave the Ecole des Beaux-Arts, and in 1899 he began to visit a small academy in the rue de Rennes where Eugène Carrière did some teaching. It was here that he met Jean Puy and Derain. The latter was living at this time at Chatou in the Seine-et-Oise department. As Vlaminck was living in the same area, the two painters eventually met (1900) and became friends. Their friendship grew rapidly, they rented a studio together near the bridge at Chatou and started to work side by side. Then, at the Van Gogh retrospective exhibition which took place in 1901 at the Bernheim-Jeune Gallery, Derain introduced Vlaminck to Matisse.

At this time, two other fauves, Dufy and Friesz, were studying at the Ecole des Beaux-Arts in Bonnat's studio. Natives of Le Havre, they too must have known each other since 1892 at least, since it was then that they began to go to evening classes at the Ecole Municipale des Beaux-Arts in their native town. Braque, who entered the same school in 1893, was also to join them in Paris at the turn of the century; and the three of them formed what was to be known as the Le Havre group. Contact with those who were to be their guides (and this is particularly true in Matisse's case) and companions at arms was established either at the dealers, or at the salons where all of them exhibited their work. It was there too that they met the Dutchman, Van Dongen, who was working in the same direction.

The dealers who backed them are quickly enumerated. There was Berthe Weill, with her little shop in the rue Victor-Massé, who received Matisse and Marquet from 1902 onwards and the majority of the others during the course of the following years. There was the Druet Gallery which opened in the rue du Faubourg Saint-Honoré in 1903. There was old Soulier, the Montmartre mattress carder, who apparently bought everything he was offered. Finally there was Vollard, but he did no more than mount one-man exhibitions for Matisse and for Van Dongen in 1904 and buy Derain's studio in 1905 and Vlaminck's in 1906.

From 1901 onwards, Matisse and Marquet also appeared at the Salon des Indépendants founded by Redon and the neo-impressionists in 1848, with the specific aim 'of allowing young artists to present their work freely to public judgment'. There was no hanging committee, and the innovators were as welcome as the traditionalists. Valtat was already exhibiting there before 1900; Manguin entered in 1902, Camoin, Dufy and Friesz in 1903, Van Dongen in 1904, Derain and Vlaminck in 1905, and Braque in 1906. However, as Maurice Denis wrote in 1908: 'For twenty-three years, the Indépendants have made a complete and conclusive trial of democracy. Everything with any pretension to the name of art has been freely and impartially exhibited. The result is now manifest. The theory of replacing the strait gate of the old-fashioned selection committee by the wide gates of freedom has, more than anything else, brought into the light all-invading mediocrity... The élite of the early days has disappeared, lost in the herd, enslaved by the exercise of liberty as it once was by academic prejudices and official hierarchy. Success has spoilt everything.' So, even before these words appeared in print, another salon had come into being, the Salon d'Automne, presided over by the architect Frantz-Jourdain, where works were once more selected by a committee. Works of daring were not by any means excluded; on the contrary, Matisse, Marquet and Valtat were represented as early as 1903. Their companions joined them during the years that followed.

At the time of the Salon des Indépendants of 1905, where Matisse, Marquet, Camoin, Manguin, Puy, Vlaminck, Derain, Friesz, Dufy and Van Dongen were to be seen, the critics chose to mention particularly the brightness of the colours and the freedom of form which were discernible in the work of some of them (although for the most part they were nowhere near true fauvism) but without referring to the existence of a group as such. This was only noticed a few months later at the Salon d'Automne, and in general it met with little critical encouragement: as in the case of other innovators who have appeared from the beginning of the nineteenth century onwards, the first appearance of the fauves was greeted with laughter and derision. They were called 'the invertebrates' or 'the incoherents'. Even the American collector Leo Stein, who bought Matisse's *Woman with Hat* (*Pl. 21*), one of the most controversial pictures, wrote in his *Appreciation* (1947): 'It was a tremendous effort on his part, a thing brilliant and powerful, but the nastiest smear of paint I had ever seen.' According to Stein, visitors hooted derisively at Matisse's works in particular, so much that the artist visited the Salon only

2 Matisse FIACRE 1900

once and his wife never dared go there at all. 'A paint-pot thrown in the public's face !' exclaimed Camille Mauclair, who elsewhere did not hesitate to write: 'As for M. Cézanne, his name will be for ever linked with the most memorable artistic joke of the last fifteen years.' For J.B. Hall, the fauve room, which some people called 'the cage', was 'the chosen room of pictorial aberration, tonal madness, the ineffable fantasies of people who, if they are not impostors, are in need of salutory academic discipline.' *L'Illustration* published on 4 November 1905 a page of reproductions of works by Matisse, Derain, Manguin, Puy, Rouault and Valtat, together with sentences taken from articles by Louis Vauxcelles, Gustave Geffroy and Thiébault-Sisson (*Pl. 4*). As Camille Mauclair wrote in *La Grande Revue* on 15 December: 'One of our illustrated contemporaries has had the amusing idea of reproducing twenty or so of the most ridiculous of these works, captioned with the flattering notices written about them by so-called "leading critics". The contrast is enough to make one die laughing.' In fact the comments reproduced in *L'Illustration* were not by any means all unalloyed praise, reserves being expressed especially with reference to the more *avant-garde* artists. Thus, while Vauxcelles saw 'the mark of a powerful personality' in Manguin, he thought that Derain was 'more a poster designer than a painter', and

3 Marquet FIACRE *c.* 1900

considered that 'his *Ships* would provide a suitable decoration for the wall of a child's bedroom'. While Geffroy remarked that 'Valtat displays real power in painting rocks, red or purplish according to the different times of day, and the bright or sombre blue of the sea', he considered that 'Matisse, otherwise so gifted, has, like others before him, strayed into eccentricities of colour from which he will doubtless return of his own accord.' But the very fact that the critics took these artists and their work seriously, that Vauxcelles should have written: 'M. Matisse is one of the most solidly gifted painters of the present day', must doubtless have seemed sufficiently grotesque in itself to the editor of *L'Illustration*.

General hostility did not prevent the artists from pursuing their own ways or from attracting another member to their band, Braque, who was registered at the Salon des Indépendants in 1906. This marks the zenith of fauvism, and for another year its fertility equalled its dynamism. Then came the decline. Already by the end of 1907 the first defections are noted, becoming more numerous; by 1908 the movement had ceased to exist. Later, I shall attempt to determine the reasons for this sudden decline. For the moment I shall simply suggest that it may have been partly due to the age of the fauves. In 1905 Matisse and Valtat were thirty-six, Manguin thirty-one, Marquet thirty, Puy and Vlaminck twenty-nine, Dufy and Van Dongen twenty-eight, Friesz and Camoin twenty-six, Derain twenty-five and Braque twenty-three. That is to say that on average they were younger than the impressionists were in 1874 but older than the *nabis* in 1890 or the cubists in 1908. In other words, for the most part they were men who had not yet turned their back on youth but who were about to do so. Hence doubtless the exuberance, the exultant vitality which characterizes fauvism, hence also perhaps the rapid cooling of certain enthusiasms, the sudden falling off of inspiration in certain cases. One should also bear in mind that some of the leaders of the movement, those who gave it its persuasive power, were, from the outset, few in number. To name Matisse, Vlaminck, Derain is to name them all. If the aim were to throw light on the essential characteristics of fauve painting one might easily confine the discussion to these three artists, and if the aim were to indicate the extremes between which it developed, one could confine the discussion to Matisse and Vlaminck. In fact, without the others fauvism would

4 Page from L'Illustration 4 November, 1905

17

have been less diversified, but essentially very little different from what it is. However, the others, especially Van Dongen, Braque, Friesz, Marquet, are not to be ignored. Not only did they contribute remarkable and idiosyncratic pictures, but without them, fauvism would not have existed as a movement.

What were its origins? In which studio can we see its first manifestations? 'Matisse and I were already working, before the 1900 Exhibition, as far back as 1898,' says Albert Marquet, 'in what was later to be called the fauve style. Our first Salon des Indépendants, where I think we were the only two painters to express ourselves in pure colours, was in 1901.' Vlaminck for his part declares that fauvism was born at Chatou and goes on to state more explicitly: 'What is fauvism? It is I, my style of that period, my manner of revolt and liberation, my rejection of academic teaching and regimentation; my blues, my reds, my yellows, my pure colours, without tonal admixtures. Derain was doubtless to some extent... infected by me.' Vlaminck elaborates this statement, going on to relate that in 1901 Matisse, accompanied by Derain, came to see him one day and that this meeting was decisive for him (Matisse). But when one compares their work, one has no difficulty in concluding that at that period Vlaminck was not more advanced than Matisse; on the contrary, he was less so. So Matisse did not need to go to Chatou to discover fauvism. One may believe him when he says: 'Derain inveigled me to go and see his family to persuade them that painting was a respectable occupation, contrary to their beliefs. And to lend importance to the occasion, I took my wife with me. Quite honestly, Derain's and Vlaminck's painting did not take me by surprise, as it was akin to my own experiments. But I was impressed to see that such very young men held convictions similar to my own'. The fact is that before meeting Vlaminck, Matisse met the work of Van Gogh, whose influence Vlaminck admits to having undergone in 1901.

It would be an exaggeration to say that at the turn of the century the painting of young artists was bound to be fauve, but it was certainly logical that it should be, since fauvism occupies a natural place in the powerful movement of artistic regeneration which developed in France after impressionism. In the first place, it was one of the last, the most violent, the most decisive assaults launched on 'official' art. But it is also a reaction against impressionism itself, which was taxed with having provided only a partial solution to the problems posed by the rejection of 'official' and traditionalist art. However, the first phases of this reaction go back as far as the 1890s.

Whilst Monet confined himself to translating the fleeting sensations of his retina into the colours of the prism, sacrificing the consistency of objects and the construction of the picture, Cézanne already aimed at 'making impressionism something solid and durable like museum art'. In his view, 'a boldly organizing mind is sensitivity's most valuable collaborator in the creation of a work of art'. Similarly, Seurat and the neo-impressionists, while continuing to record phenomena of light, laid emphasis on carefully worked-out construction. In order to retain freshness and brilliance of colour they applied their paint in dots or in little squares, according to a 'precise and scientific method' whose principles are explained by Paul Signac in 1899 in his treatise *D'Eugène Delacroix au Néo-Impressionnisme*. Gauguin's criticism of Monet and his companions was harsher. In his opinion, the impressionists produced 'a purely superficial art, nothing but coquetry, purely materialist, devoid of thought'. He concluded that it was vital to make a radical break with them. The only thing he did not reject was their palette, but he considered that it should be used in a different spirit. He remarked, 'It is said that God took a handful of clay, and we all know what he made from it. The artist in his turn (if he really wants to achieve the divine creative act), should not so much copy nature as take the elements of nature and create a new element from them.' Van Gogh's attitude is similar to that of Gauguin. In his letters to his brother Théo he writes, 'I don't know if I can paint the postman *as I feel him*' (and not: as I see him). And elsewhere, 'Instead of trying to render what I see before me, I use colour in a completely arbitrary way in order to express myself powerfully'. And in this sentence he defined fauvism fifteen years before its appearance. Following the advice of Cézanne and Gauguin, and also of Odilon Redon, who had himself constantly held out against these 'real parasites of the object' that the impressionists were in his eyes, the *nabis* also attempted, in the words of Maurice Denis, 'to translate emotions and concepts through formal correspondences'. Moreover, some of them used vivid colours; Vuillard in particular, who was later to opt for subdued tones, occasionally chose around 1890-1 to express himself in pure tones applied in flat tints, thus creating works which, had they appeared in 1905, would naturally have been classified as fauve.

However, if the above-mentioned painters were the precursors of fauvism, its appearance at the beginning of the century was nonetheless the outcome of a series of battles fought and won. Human logic and the logic of history do not spontaneously coincide; the originators of the movement did not find their way immediately. Neither did they all find it in the same manner, nor, when they had found it, did they all go at the same speed or with the same clear sense of purpose. So, before trying to determine what they have in common, it is as well to discuss the individual characteristics of each: what particular forms his experiments took, and in what respect his development was distinctive.

Rouault is sometimes classified as a fauve, doubtless because he too had been a pupil of Gustave Moreau and had exhibited at the Salon d'Automne of 1905, being reviled like his colleagues, and because one of his works was reproduced on the special page of *L'Illustration*. However, his moral preoccupations, his dominating expressionist tendencies, and especially his continuing attachment for *chiaroscuro*, exclude him from the ranks of the fauves properly speaking. For this reason it seems natural not to include him in this book.

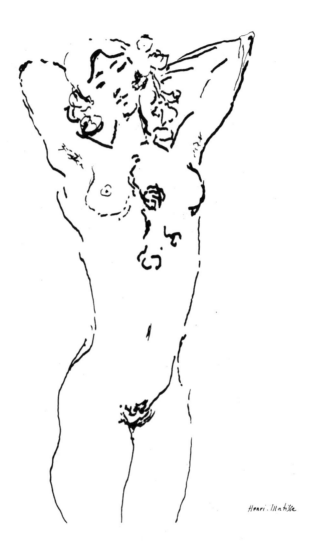

Henri. Matisse

The Fauve Painters

6 Matisse STUDIO OF GUSTAVE MOREAU 1895

Henri Matisse In Gustave Moreau's studio, Matisse was first of all, according to a fellow-pupil, Henri Evenepoel, a 'painter of refinement, with a skilful mastery of greys'. A canvas of 1894-5, showing Moreau's studio at the Ecole des Beaux-Arts *(Pl. 6)*, confirms this judgment. A complete absence of vivid tones, simply a somewhat cold grisaille gently warmed in places with a little yellow ochre. A whitish stroke here and there, while elsewhere the grey becomes darker, turning to black. A subdued light falls on a female nude model posing in the foreground and a statue in the background, touching almost furtively a few students standing before their easels, making them into darkened silhouettes. Nowhere does Matisse draw figures or objects with precision; he has obviously no desire to linger over details, nor does he concern himself with the anecdotal aspect: it is not his aim to depict a picturesque scene but to create a pictorial reality, to follow the graduations of this subdued light as it encounters the bodies and reverberates from one to the other. The attention he pays to the effects of light, as well as

7
Matisse
Copy of Raphael's
BALDASSARE CASTIGLIONE
c. 1894

the veiled appearance he gives to objects may seem reminiscent of impressionism, from which he is however far removed from the point of view of colour. The spiritual climate of this picture is distinguished by its calm: no gesticulation, no exchange of words; the human beings are no less silent than the objects and the bare walls. In this respect, the work is already quite characteristic, although the artist's style is still dominated by traditional rules.

During the years 1895 to 1900, Matisse used to visit the Louvre in order to make copies of paintings. His choice of works is indicative of his continued preoccupation with the problem of tonal values: still-lifes by David de Heem *(The Dessert)*, and Chardin *(The Skate, The Pipe, Pyramid of Fruit, Still-life, Fruit and Vegetables, Still-life with Red Lacquer Table)*, as well as Philippe de Champaigne's *Dead Christ,* Raphael's *Baldassare Castiglione (Pl. 7)*, some compositions by Poussin *(Bacchante, The Bunch of Grapes)*, by Carracci, Watteau, Fragonard... and finally Delacroix's *Rape of Rebecca ;* Matisse has completely transposed this canvas, where the reds and blues are so eloquent, into black and white.

However, on Belle-Ile in 1896, he came into contact with the Australian painter John Russell, who knew Monet and Van Gogh personally and who guided him towards a conception of painting which is based on colour. He now began to do landscapes akin to those of the impressionists. Two years later in Corsica he painted the *Little Olive Trees,* evocative of Renoir, but a Renoir with a broader, more passionate, less caressing touch, the tones less inclined to melt into each other. The frenzied brushwork and vividness of colouring are more marked in a landscape of 1898-9, *The Countryside around Toulouse (Pl. 9):* here Matisse is nearer to Van Gogh than to Renoir. One may wonder whether the new force of his colouring was suggested to him by the subject or simply by his palette. Doubtless the southern landscape called forth harmonies which a less brilliant sunlight would not have evoked. However, 1898 marks the appearance of other pictures which are notable for the purity of their colour composition. A *Nude in the Studio* (Bridgestone Museum, Tokyo) is stippled with red (for the body) and green (for the background); and this treatment, influenced by neo–impressionism, clearly shows a desire to construct a picture purely by means of colour. There is, in effect, little definition of form; the body is not sharply distinguished from the background and any difference there

8
Matisse
CORSICAN LANDSCAPE
1898

9 Matisse THE COUNTRYSIDE AROUND TOULOUSE 1898–9

is, is due less to the flattened volume than to the contrast of colours. *A Still-life against the Light* of 1899 gives a more three-dimensional effect, particularly an effect of distance. But the colour, which is now spread in fairly large areas, is yet more pure and more intense *(Pl. 10)*. There is something overheated in these orange tones, these reds, and lilacs, and athough they are challenged by blues, greens and purples, the warm shades clearly predominate. What is more, it is not only the vibrancy of the colouring which is striking, it is also its unusual quality, the daring choice of tones and their juxtaposition which arrests one's attention. It is not at all surprising, then, that critics confronted with this sort of work have spoken of pre-fauvism: the use made of colour here clearly prefigures the role it was to assume in the fauve period.

Subsequent pictures, like the *Interior with Harmonium (Pl. 11)* and the *Nude with Pink Shoes (Pl. 12)* show Matisse wrestling with the problem of form rather than colour. He had realized that both are equally important and that he should apply himself to evolving not only new colour harmonies but also a new technique of draughtsmanship. The *Nude* is particularly revealing in this respect: it looks as though it has been shaped out of wood with a knife. His modelling is summary: the planes of light and shade are somewhat crudely opposed. The artist's attempt to free himself from academic form, and even a certain straining after effect, are clearly discernible; one can see too that he has profited from studying Cézanne. Pissarro, whom he met from time to time, had revealed Cézanne's merits to him and he had bought one of his pictures, the *Three Bathers,* several months before. Although his means were at this time strictly limited, he had not been able to resist the temptation to buy this work from Vollard's; and he was to keep it lovingly until 1934, when he donated it to the Petit Palais in Paris. But he had not studied Cézanne only, he had in addition bought a small *Head of a Boy* by Gauguin; and the range of colour in his *Nude with Pink Shoes* is more reminiscent of Gauguin than of Cézanne. Apparently, Matisse wanted to own a Van Gogh, but his financial position obliged him to give up the idea.

10 Matisse STILL-LIFE AGAINST THE LIGHT 1899

He did, however, manage to buy two pastel drawings by Redon which must have attracted him by the importance which the artist gives to the imagination in his work and by the unreal, poetic and rarefied quality of the colouring.

The danger of looking on such disparate masters for guidance is that the artist may sacrifice something of his own individuality. Matisse, however, believed that in his own case this was a means of strengthening it. 'I have never shunned outside influences', he once told Jacques Guenne, 'I should have considered that to be an act of cowardice and bad faith towards myself. I believe that the struggles

which an artist undergoes help him to assert his personality. One
would have to be very naïve not to look and see what direction other
people are working in. I am surprised that people can be so little
concerned about themselves and their work as to believe that they
have hit upon the truth of their art from the very outset. I happen to
have accepted influences. But I think that I have always been able to
master them.'

From 1901 to 1904, he advanced cautiously. Looking at certain
works of this period (the *Carmelina* for instance, *Pl. 14*) one even
has the impression that he has gone back on earlier progress. His

colour has darkened and he has begun to take account of the play of light and shade once again. Should one conclude from this that he doubted the value of earlier experiments and the pre-fauve works of 1898 to 1901 of which they are the outcome? It seems more probable that he wanted a time for rest and reflection. Indeed, if he never baulked at a venture, he never committed himself without being certain that he had sufficient strength to overcome obstacles.

Moreover, he did not completely give up expressing himself in primary colours, as is proved by his *Notre-Dame* (1900-4). In the pictures which treat this subject with the greatest freedom, not only is the colouring vivid, but it bears little relation to the outside world

13
Matisse
NUDE PUTTING UP HAIR
1901

14
Matisse
CARMELINA
1903

(*Pl. 16*). The waters of the Seine show uninhibited greens, purples, reds and orange tones next to blues and greyish ochres. The façade of the cathedral is decked out in mauve and lilac; streaks of green emphasizing the vertical quality of the towers. The steeply falling perspective of these pictures reminds one of Marquet, which is not at all surprising seeing that the two friends lived in the same house—19 Quai Saint-Michel—and worked together from time to time. In the last analysis, they are both indebted for this perspective to Japanese prints, which had exercised a more or less strong influence on

15 Matisse PONT SAINT-MICHEL 1900

French painting from the impressionists onwards. 'What a lesson
in harmony, purity I gained from those prints,' Matisse was to say
later. He was also to recall the large-scale exhibition of Islamic art
which was put on at the Pavillon de Marsan in 1903. But, however
strong the impression it made on him, it did not lead him to 'orien-
talize' his painting or even appreciably to modify his style.

     This was to be effected by another meeting: in 1904 Matisse spent
the summer at Saint-Tropez, where Paul Signac had a villa and where
Henri-Edmond Cross, who was living nearby at Le Lavandou, used
to come and visit him. The three artists met, and if Matisse was not
immediately won over to the neo-impressionist beliefs of his elders,
he certainly showed no hostility to them. Take for instance the
View of Saint-Tropez (Pl. 17), where reds and orange tones abound
and where the handling often has a 'tachist' quality, a quality which
became more apparent in the works which he did in Paris during the
winter of 1904-5. One of them shows *Marquet Painting a Nude
(Pl. 18)*, and this canvas, which we shall later compare with its

16
Matisse
NOTRE–DAME
1902

17 Matisse VIEW OF SAINT-TROPEZ 1904

companion piece *Matisse Painting a Nude* by Marquet *(Pl. 93)*, shows that neo-impressionism had really allowed Matisse to liberate his colours and free himself from traditional form. In 1929 he was to tax neo-impressionism with being 'an often mechanical method related to a purely physical emotion', and still later he was to tell Gaston Diehl that he had experienced great difficulty in conforming to 'divisionist' principles. The fact is that he concentrated less on a scientific interpretation of light than on a lyrical expression of colour. The radiance of his picture was more important to him than the naturalistic representation of light. Furthermore, surely one of his reasons for turning to the neo-impressionists was their preoccu-

18
Matisse
Study for
MARQUET PAINTING
A NUDE 1904-5

19
Matisse
PASTORAL
1905

20
Matisse
OLIVE TREES
1905

21
Matisse
WOMAN WITH HAT
1905

pation with decorative composition and their preference for method-
ical working? However that may be, the following passage by
Paul Signac in his book *D'Eugène Delacroix au Néo-impressionnisme*
might very well have been written by Matisse: 'The indiscriminate
placing of reds, greens, yellows side by side does not make one a
colourist. One must know how to order these disparate elements,
to sacrifice some in order to set off the others to better advantage.'
When in 1904-5 he painted a large pointillist picture depicting nudes
on the beach at Saint-Tropez *(Pl. 25)*, he was concerned not only
with luminosity but also to a larger extent with the decorative
arrangement of colour. Moreover, if the theme of the nude or the
group of nudes in a landscape was dear to him, it was obviously
partly on account of its sensual aspect and partly on account of the

arabesques, the rhythmic forms which it allowed him to depict on the canvas. Standing, seated or lying on a Mediterranean shore, the bathers are primarily forms covered in multiple blocks of colours, rather than nudes. And these forms appear enclosed by swaying, complementary curves, contrasting with the straight vertical line of a pine tree to the right, harmonizing with the undulations of the coastline rising obliquely to the left. Remembering the incantatory refrain of Baudelaire's poem *Invitation au Voyage*,

> *Là, tout n'est qu'ordre et beauté,*
> *Luxe, calme et volupté,*

> 'There all is order and beauty,
> Luxury, calm and delight',

Matisse took *Luxe, calme et volupté* as the title of a painting which Signac liked so much at the Salon des Indépendants of 1905 that he bought it on the spot: he hung it at his villa at Saint–Tropez and kept it for the rest of his life *(Pl. 25)*.

Matisse on the other hand was about to abandon neo–impressionism. From late spring and throughout the summer he stayed at Collioure and brought back with him canvases such as *Woman with Hat* and *Open Window* which were to figure some months later in the fauve room at the Salon d'Automne and which were to be reproduced on the famous page of *L'Illustration* of 4 November *(Pl. 4)*.

'I have faith that a new school of colourists will take root in the Midi', Van Gogh had written to his brother Théo in 1888. It so happened that the Midi fired and enriched the work of several exponents of fauvism: Derain, Friesz, Braque, as well as Matisse. But it was Matisse who drew from it the richest, the rarest, the most original brilliance. This time there is no doubt about it: the colours the artist

23 Matisse Study for THE JOY OF LIVING 1905

24 Matisse The Joy of Living 1905-6

brings into play are taken from his palette and not from nature. These pinks, mauves, and bluish greens, these bright reds, oranges, purples, these pale or fully saturated blues, all these are colours which are invented rather than observed. They are no longer applied in spots but in patches, filling greater or smaller areas: and their harmonies have a flavour which on first encounter is strange and pungent, becoming progressively more complex, more fascinating and heady, born from the marriage of sensory intelligence and daring imagination. Thus their aim is not to reproduce the appearance of the visible world, but to transpose by means of colour the artist's sensations in the presence of nature. Besides, the colours relate to the demands of pictorial composition; and this also may have the effect of removing them from visible reality.

Form in these works is now simply indicated in bold strokes. It is suggested rather than defined; sometimes there is an interval be-

25 Matisse LUXE, CALME ET VOLUPTÉ 1904-5

tween form and ground where the canvas is left white, making a halo
in which the objects seem to float, and creating a narrow zone of
calm between the colours which dulls their impact.   One might
almost say that the painter hesitates to define the form for fear of
falling back into conventional patterns again; this is a common
phenomenon with an artist who is seeking to establish his identity.
Although he is perfectly sure of what he does not want, he is less
sure about what he is going to put in the place of what he is challeng-
ing; or he has the knowledge but not yet the means of expressing it.
Hence the presence of a categorical tone in the rejection which is
absent from the affirmation.

What Matisse was rejecting, where form was concerned, was the
depiction of volume by relief, the gradual transition from light to

dark. Henceforward he was to express it in terms of colour, or at least try to do so, without diminishing the vitality of the latter. Two solutions presented themselves to him. The impressionists had replaced *chiaroscuro* by using warm tones for the lighted parts of objects, and cold tones for those parts which were in shadow; following the Japanese example, Gauguin and Van Gogh, however, had preferred the technique of outlining forms so that the direction of the contour suggested movement and at the same time enclosed a colour which was all the more vivid because it was flat and even. The Matisse of 1905 used these two techniques: the first can be seen in *Woman with Hat (Pl. 21)*, the second in *Portrait with Green Streak (Pl. 151)*.

Moreover, in *Woman with Hat,* Matisse did not simply borrow the new impressionist technique of depicting light and shade: he placed his colours with a freedom which his predecessors' naturalism would have found unacceptable. His palette is deliberately 'artificial': a brick-red head of hair under a hat in which reds, mauves, blues and greens are juxtaposed. An orange-coloured neck above a dress

26
Matisse
Study for
Luxe, calme
et volupté
1904

41

which repeats the colours of the hat, differently combined and accen‐
tuated. In more muted form, they appear again in the background
which relates neither to an object nor to a room, but is simply a
painted surface, the paint put on in a manner which is as broad as it
is generous. The effect of all this is a colour composition which is
flowery rather than mottled, vivid and sparkling rather than garish.

In the *Portrait with Green Streak,* two zones of colour, almost flat
tints which a skilful brushwork makes vibrant, divide the face evenly:
on the left, an ochre zone and on the right a pink zone. A yellowish‐
green line divides them from the forehead to the chin; and it is this
line especially which produces the illusion of three dimensions.
Other features of this work will be touched on later; for the present,
one need only mention the original way in which Matisse suggests
volume.

The *Open Window (Pl. 22)* provides an example of the way Matisse was treating problems of space in 1905. Although the colours which are found in the foreground are echoed in the background, they are less closely knit, more lightly distributed. In other words, Matisse still respected aerial perspective to a certain extent. He also continued to make use of linear perspective, although he no longer troubled to make the different lines converge on a single vanishing point; in short, he remained fundamentally faithful to the notation of space formulated by the Italian Renaissance, whilst exercising a great deal of freedom in its application. He lessened the impression of depth, so that the colour might be pure and brilliant throughout the painting: *The Siesta (Pl. 33),* also painted at Collioure, demonstrates his aim even better than the *Open Window.*

In 1906 he completed a vast composition which he called *The Joy of Living:* sixteen nudes, for the most part women, resting, embracing

28
Matisse
NUDE
1906

or dancing in an idyllic landscape *(Pls. 5, 23, 24)*. Although the theme is fairly close to that of *Luxe, calme et volupté (Pls. 25, 26)* the same cannot be said of the style, which denotes a marked influence of Gauguin, a series of whose works from the South Sea Islands Matisse had seen during his stay at Collioure. They were at this time in the keeping of a friend of Gauguin's, Daniel de Monfreid, who was living at Corneille-en-Conflans, near Collioure, and it was through the good offices of the sculptor Maillol that Matisse had the opportunity of viewing them on several occasions. Then again, *The Joy of Living* shows several affinities with oriental art. The form is defined with a clear contour, and the colour is applied almost everywhere in flat tints. Never before had Matisse used the arabesque more resolutely; ample and flexible, it defines trees as well as human figures; line alone constructs bodies and gives them the appearance

29
Matisse
SEATED NUDE
1906

30
Matisse
MARGOT
1907

of volume. The stroke is heavy or fine and cursive according to whether they are standing against a light or dark background. The placing of the nudes marks the different planes, but their height is not always relative to their position in space, because the painter is less concerned with giving the impression of reality than with composing the elements of his picture; he alters nature so as to make pictorial form more harmonious and more expressive. If, like Ingres, who had laid himself open to the charge of having painted an *Odalisque* with 'three vertebrae too many', he lengthens the body of the nude who is seen from the rear in the middle distance, it is because he wants both to emphasize the horizontal line and to indicate the gentle relaxation which is the theme of the picture.

Various figures from *The Joy of Living* were to reappear in the works which Matisse completed in the next few years. In 1909–10 he singled out the circle of female dancers from the background, and, cutting down their numbers from six to five, and increasing their height, he created the vast composition known as *The Dance* *(Pl. 203)*. As far back as 1907 the nude standing on the left, as well as the one bending before her, had appeared in a slightly different form in *Luxury,* a painting of three nudes on a beach. There are two versions of this work, just as there are two versions of *The Young Sailor* which Matisse painted a year earlier *(Pl. 36)*. The first *Luxury* *(Pl. 34)* shows the artist still unsure in places how to handle his theme. In the standing nude in the foreground, here and there the contour has been gone over several times and thickened in the artist's attempt to correct himself. On the other hand, this nude is not entirely free from realism, apart from the breasts, which are stylized to the point of being schematic. Finally, although each colour occupies a quite clearly defined area, it is not usually applied complete-ly pure, but is shaded, modulated. In the final version *(Pl. 35)* all these hesitations disappear. Everywhere the colour is applied in flat

31 Matisse STILL-LIFE WITH RED CARPET 1906

32 Matisse MARGUERITE READING 1906

tints, except in the purple mountain in the background where some shading persists. The draughtsmanship, which has lost both whatever schematic elements it had and what realism it still retained, has become refined, sinuous and vibrant, defining the bodies with precision and sensitivity. We should observe, too, that the picture is not lacking in depth. By cutting down the dimensions of the third nude and interposing the mountains, the artist gives us a positive feeling of space and at the same time, through his use of flat tints, accentuates the flat character of the canvas.

However, Matisse's experiments between 1906 and 1907 were not confined to those we have just discussed. Pictures in which colours are used in an even, homogeneous way alternate with those in which the flat tints give place to a varied surface of coloured strokes. The latter are the descendants of the *Woman with Hat* of 1905 *(Pl. 21)*, and amongst them we should mention *The Gipsy* of 1906 *(Pl. 27)*. The colouring here possesses even more brilliance than in the

Collioure canvas. The treatment seems even more spontaneous; at least the painter is even more anxious to give it the free and easy appearance of a first sketch. The face and the naked torso of *The Gipsy*, with its confronting and contrasting green and pink, blue and orange, yellow and lilac, are in danger of seeming striped, so great is Matisse's daring in his choice of colours, in the way he places them and the somewhat aggressive accent he gives them. Certainly, few of his pictures of that period are more irreverent towards the notions of reality of 'good taste' (which is often merely pusillanimous taste): few of his pictures are more 'highly-seasoned' or more fascinating. By comparison with this picture, which gives the impression that the artist has decided to break free from convention to an extent bordering on the impertinent, the *Blue Nude—Souvenir of Biskra* of 1907 *(Pl. 40)* seems extremely moderate. However, distortions are not lacking; whilst vigorously outlining the body, Matisse does not abstain from marking in several shadings with rapid blue strokes.

In addition to the works in which the human figure is the central theme and where the landscape, if present, is a mere background *(Boy with Butterfly Net, Pl. 41)*, Matisse did some pure landscapes: *Brook with Aloes* for instance (private collection, Houston, Texas) and *The Bank (Pl. 38)*. In these canvases of 1907, spatial depth is only vaguely perceptible and the artist takes almost no account of the effect of distance on the colour. He certainly wanted to suggest the motive which inspired him, but his primary purpose was that each colour should be clear and unsullied, wherever it was placed and whatever plane it was intended to indicate.

Matisse adopts the same techniques in painting interiors and still-lifes. Moreover, there are, amongst the latter, some highly significant works which demonstrate the artist's refusal to adopt one formula exclusively. The *Still-life with Red Carpet* of 1906 *(Pl. 31)* is distinguished by richness of tonal harmonies: everything in it tends to amplify the shimmering quality of the surfaces, the variety of the textures and the versatility of the handling. But the *Pink Onions* of 1906 *(Pl. 37)* on the other hand offers muted tonalities and rare harmonies.

If one compares these canvases of the fauve period with the *Still-life against the Light* of 1899 *(Pl. 10)*, one can see that here as elsewhere Matisse's experiments are not directed simply at solving

33 Matisse THE SIESTA (INTERIOR AT COLLIOURE) 1905

problems of colour. In the earlier work, the notation of space and the layout of the composition are still conventional and the form is stylized rather than recreated. In other words, apart from the colour, the painter's conception remains fundamentally realistic. In the still-lifes of 1906, however, we are confronted not only with a new palette but with a new vision, which, far from ignoring material reality, gives it a different weight, a different factual significance, in short, a more striking appearance. So, although Matisse broke with realism, he did not break with reality. And although he was seeking synthetic form, he always used nature as his starting point, which is why one sometimes finds him apparently going back on earlier progress. In effect, he was simply making contact with the ground again, the better to spring off on a subsequent occasion.

Any art which stylizes nature runs the risk of becoming cold and schematic; Matisse knew this too well not to forearm himself against this danger by ever–renewed contact with material reality. He knew too that art is a transposition, and he constantly strove towards a more and more condensed transposition.

He himself acknowledged this in a well-known article in *La Grande Revue* of 25 December 1908. We read: 'Often, when I start to work, I notice new and superficial sensations at the first sitting. Some years ago, this result was sometimes enough for me. If I were satisfied with that now that I think I can see further, my picture would

36 Matisse THE YOUNG SAILOR 1906

seem to remain somehow incomplete; I would have recorded the
fleeting sensations of a moment in time which is not representative
of my whole personality, and which I would scarcely recognize the
following day. I want to achieve that state of condensation of
sensations which makes a picture. I could be satisfied with a work

37
Matisse
PINK ONIONS
1906

38
Matisse
THE BANK
1907

completed from the first sketch, but I should subsequently tire of it, and I prefer to touch up a work so that I can recognize it later as a representation of my mind. There was a time when I never hung my canvases on the wall for any length of time because they reminded me of states of overstimulation, which, in calmer mood, I didn't like to see. Nowadays, I try to infuse some calm into my pictures and I keep working at them until I have succeeded in doing so.

'I think one can judge an artist's power and vitality by his ability, when intimately moved by a natural scene, to order his impressions to the point where he can come back and continue working on them on several occasions and on different days: such a power implies a

39
Matisse
MUSIC
1907

40 Matisse Blue Nude – Souvenir of Biskra 1907

man so far master of himself that he can impose a discipline on himself.'

But can a kind of painting which involves so much reflection be classified as fauve ? If fauvism is a mere spontaneous outpouring, then obviously such meditated works as Matisse's do not belong to this category; and in this case Matisse was a fauve only at the beginning of his stay at Collioure, because it was only during that period that he gave free rein to his impulses. Is this to say that he should not be included among the fauves ? On the contrary, we are bound to see in him the most consistent of the fauves, the one who most fully understood the problems confronting the movement; what is more, he remained a fauve until his death, whilst, as we have already mentioned, his companions of the early days quickly abandoned the fight. If therefore we leave him at this juncture it is because we have reached the moment which marks the end of fauvism as a movement, for, as we shall see later, as far as Matisse was concerned, there was no break between what he painted in 1907 and what he was to paint in 1910 and even in 1935 and 1950.

41 Matisse BOY WITH BUTTERFLY NET 1907

Maurice de Vlaminck Vlaminck's fauvism, unlike Matisse's, is in no way the result of a slow process of maturation; it seems rather to explode like a rocket. Vehement, turbulent, aggressive, it was dominated not by reflection and critical intelligence but by the dictates of Vlaminck's impulsive nature and unbridled instincts. Indeed, whereas Matisse stated: 'Instinct must be thwarted just as one prunes the branches of a tree so that it will grow better,' Vlaminck exclaims, 'It takes more courage to follow one's instincts than to die a hero's death on the field of battle.' Whereas Matisse had admitted that he had 'never avoided outside influences,' and that he had always compared his experiments with those of his predecessors, Vlaminck proclaims: 'Visiting museums bastardizes the personality, just as hobnobbing with priests makes you lose your faith.' He goes

on to say: 'I have never "thought about art", classical art, Italian art,
the Greeks. I wanted to burn the Ecole des Beaux-Arts with my
cobalts and vermilions and I wanted to interpret my feelings with
my brushes without thinking about what had gone on before in
painting. I don't "think about art", I want to show how I like a
thing or how I hate an established order. When I get my hands on
painting materials I don't give a damn about other people's painting:

44
Vlaminck
QUAI SGANZIN
AT NANTERRE
1902

45
Vlaminck
POND AT
SAINT-CUCUFA
c. 1902-3

life and me, me and life. In art, every generation must start again afresh.'

This splendid profession of faith should not be taken too literally. Vlaminck did not make an entirely fresh start; any more than anyone else. He did not invent his style independently of all outside influences; and to say this is in no way to reproach him but simply to point out that in the last resort he was less exceptional than he was pleased to believe.

His works are for the most part undated, so it is not at all easy to retrace his development; a task which is made all the more difficult by the fact the dates given by his biographers often do not tally with each other. One gives the date 1905 to a canvas which, according to

46
Vlaminck
KITCHEN INTERIOR
1904

47 Vlaminck GARDENS AT CHATOU 1904

another, must have been done around 1900, and according to a third,
in 1902. A work which we are told in one place was painted in 1906
is given elsewhere as dating from 1907. These facts are significant:
they prove how little Vlaminck changed during the course of his
fauve period. When did this begin? One of his earliest works is a
canvas of 1900 entitled *The Bar Counter (Pl. 51):* a coarse, blue-eyed
girl with ochre and vermilion hair and heavy body encased in a white
blouse is standing insolently behind a glass of red wine. The violence
of these colours as well as the weighty and passionate treatment of
the subject clearly herald fauvism. In another picture of 1900, *Man
with Red Scarf,* also called *Le Père Bouju* or *Man with a Pipe (Pl. 42),*
the manner seems even more frenzied, with an element of madness;
the pigments are thick, the draughtsmanship rudimentary, not to
say crude; and all this too augurs the works of 1905 to 1907. How-

48 Vlaminck ROAD AT MARLY-LE-ROI 1905-6

ever, apart from the scarf, the colours in this picture are far from being pure and vivid.

Vlaminck's palette needed to come in contact with Van Gogh's sun before it could catch fire. Even so, the fire did not break out immediately. His discovery of Van Gogh, one will remember, took place at the Bernheim-Jeune Gallery in 1901, but the effect of this only became fully apparent a couple of years later. Indeed, the drawing and the brushwork of the *Little Girl with Doll* of 1902 *(Pl. 43)* are tame by comparison with the *Man with Red Scarf*. The same comment holds good for landscape like the *Quai Sganzin at Nanterre (Pl. 44)*, or the *Pond at Saint-Cucufa (Pl. 45)* whose dates are given as 1902 or 1903. The first of these canvases displays heavily emphasized outlines with a predominance of long horizontal lines and a somewhat lifelessly applied colouring which is muted and even hesitant in parts. The second has more fire, but not much more vigour in its colour composition. Nevertheless, Vlaminck was swept

49 Vlaminck BARGE 1905

off his feet by Van Gogh's exhibition at the Bernheim–Jeune Gallery –
as he confided later: 'That day, I loved Van Gogh more than my
own father.'

What was it that he loved in Van Gogh? When one remembers
the sort of thing that Van Gogh wrote to his brother Théo, for
instance the following sentence: 'So don't think that I should keep
myself in a state of fevered excitement without a valid reason, but
you must realize that I am in the middle of a complicated calculation,
whose results are a series of pictures done in quick succession, speed-
ily executed but thought out a long time *in advance*', then one is
somewhat surprised to learn that, according to M. Maurice Genevoix, Vlaminck hailed in Van Gogh the creator of an art 'which
posed no problems'. The important thing is that this was how
Vlaminck saw Van Gogh: a man unfolding his heart to us, confes-
sing, emancipating himself unrestrainedly, candidly, guilelessly. And
that is how Vlaminck wished to be himself. An enemy of all rules

and regulations which others might seek to impose on him, thirsting for liberty (witness his contributing articles and poems to *Anarchie* in about 1900 and to *Libertaire,* which put him in bad odour with the police), a passionate and unjust champion (in his books) of what he considered to be justice and moral health. He had only one aim: to express himself as directly as possible, to be brutally frank rather than to lack sincerity. His physical strength, which was exceptional, impelled him to violence as well. He was a champion cyclist at twenty-one and spent several years as a professional; he was a successful oarsman as well.

We see him painting in 1904 a *Kitchen Interior (Pl. 46)* where a purplish window and a red floor contrast with acid greens and light or dark blues. An air of disquiet emanates from the harshness of these harmonies. An uneasiness seems to manifest itself. In any case, we do not find here that feeling of relaxation and well-being suggested by Matisse's *Interior at Collioure (The Siesta, Pl. 33)* of the following

50 Vlaminck VILLAGE 1906

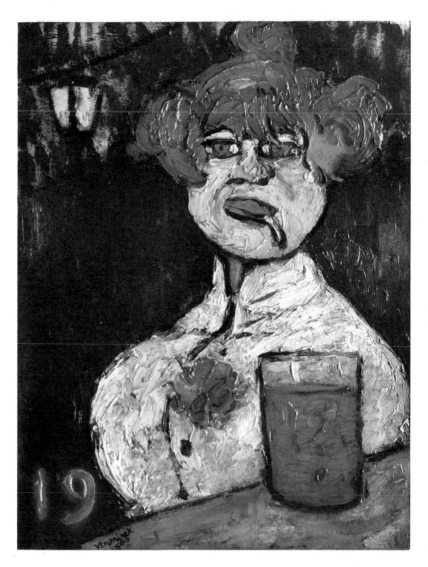

year although this too is expressed in terms of the opposition of warm and cold tones.

Even more than in the *Kitchen Interior,* Vlaminck's fauvism becomes fully apparent in the landscapes which he painted in 1904–7. Whether ·he took *Gardens at Chatou (Pl. 47)*, *Red Trees (Pl. 55)*, *Bateaux-Lavoirs (Pl. 58)*, *The Barge (Pl. 49)* or *The Seine at Carrières-sur-Seine (Pl. 54)*, he constantly threw glowing, fiery colours on to his canvases. And as he juxtaposes them with fierce passion, in a lusty, intense, sensual subject, his pictures call to mind fanfares and sometimes deafening fairground music. Yellows, blues and reds crowd in front of red and green *bateaux-lavoirs* ; grasses of flam-boyant orange stand out in profile against a Seine in which greens and cobalts, yellows and vermilions jostle each other. The wild disordered branches of some of his trees have become mere tongues of fire drawn out or torn to shreds by the wind. The tree trunks are flowing streams of bright or brownish red interspersed with green, blue or purplish streaks. Some streets have the appearance of braziers fanned by a wind of inexhaustible violence. In other words, there is, in general, a complete absence of joyfulness in Vlaminck's painting, notwithstanding their vivid quality. There is no question of man's being able to contemplate nature with serene pleasure in his works. Whereas for the impressionists the Seine was a shining mirror of delight, here the reflections smite the eye painfully rather than caress

52 Vlaminck PICNIC 1905

53
Vlaminck
DANCER
AT THE ' RAT MORT '
1906

it. Sturdy tugs running against the stream, high factory chimneys rising on either bank help to destroy the bucolic character of these landscapes. Even when only two yachts are to be seen on the blue surface, the scene lacks the peaceful aspect presented by a similar subject painted by Monet. The boats do not glide gently on the serene waters; their progress has to contend with wind and fast-flowing currents. Impatience and violent emotion are to be found in almost every one of these works; this atmosphere is no less characteristic of the painter than is the stridency of his colouring.

Moreover, in spite of the intensity of his colours, Vlaminck remains closer to nature than Matisse. As a rule, he confines himself

54 Vlaminck THE SEINE AT CARRIÈRES-SUR-SEINE 1906

to heightening the colours presented by visible reality, replacing
brown with red and orange, grey with blue and yellow. He indicates
shadow sometimes with a cold shade, sometimes with a warm one,
darker than the colours used for the lighter part of the form. Sometimes he dispenses with shadow entirely. Since he does not generally
use continuous outlines, his volumes are often somewhat flattened.

On the whole, his colour composition is more ordinary than
Matisse's or Derain's. This is because instead of making up thinned
colours on his palette, Vlaminck works 'with paint squeezed direct on
to the canvas'. His aim is to express strength, not delicate refinement,
although he does occasionally achieve the latter. In addition, he is
often in too much of a hurry to express his feelings to be able to
linger over refinements of language. The same reason doubtless
also explains why he takes so little trouble with his draughtsmanship.
Whether his lines are slow and deliberate or rapid, he is always heavy,
schematic and inexpressive; he confines himself to defining and
suggesting objects. Rarely has his line any life of its own. His

55 Vlaminck RED TREES 1906

manner, on the other hand, is not lacking in eloquence; if the desired
effect is to depict a relative stability (in land surfaces or tree trunks
for instance), the brushstroke is fairly expressive, following the
direction of the horizontal or the vertical. If, on the other hand, he
wants to express movement (quivering grasses, gesticulating arms)
when painting the *Dancer at the 'Rat Mort'* (*Pl. 53*) or a *Picnic* (*Pl. 52*)
with a couple on the brink of passion, his hand dashes off regular,
parallel strokes of colour in a diagonal direction or makes them
undulate, dance, whirl round. In every case the manner corresponds
to the feelings which it is his aim to transcribe. The tumultuous
elements in his nature lead him naturally to prefer dots, juxtaposed
or even superimposed, to the flat tint. But this does not mean that
he completely does away with flat tints: a notable instance of his use
of them is the *Village* of 1906 (*Pl. 50*), which is one of his most
intense and best constructed pictures.

Vlaminck is so obsessed with colour that he occasionally applies
it without considering whether the object which it represents will

retain its consistency and its unity; this accounts for his painting tree trunks on which an ochre orange zone is placed above a vermilion zone, and the first appears more distant than the second, although it is meant to be situated on the same plane.

This artist's works are not meant to be examined too closely. They are more striking through an overall impression of power, vigour and fire than through the accuracy of their detail. Compared with Matisse's art, Vlaminck's is not only unpolished, it is crude: an art which bellows and roars rather than sings, carrying one along by its common touch, its verve and generosity, its frank and primitive quality, by the often frenzied passion with which it approaches, embraces and glorifies the world, but which leaves in the mind a sense of incompleteness which mere physical things cannot dispel.

Unlike Matisse, who never ceased to examine his work and to go back over what he had done, Vlaminck was completely spontaneous, only ever working from the first sketch. 'I have never worked,' he said; 'I have painted. I have tried to exploit a natural gift to the full.

56 Vlaminck BATHERS 1907

57 Vlaminck THE LOCK AT BOUGIVAL 1908

My object was to get to know myself through and through, my qualities and my faults.' In other words, to him painting was merely a means, whereas for Matisse it was an end in itself. Vlaminck was fully aware of this. 'Painting was an abscess which drained off the evil in me. Without a gift for painting I would have gone to the bad... What I could only have achieved in a social context by throwing a bomb—which would have led one to the scaffold—I have tried to express in art, in painting, by using pure colours straight from the tube. Thus I have been able to use my destructive instincts in order to recreate a sensitive, living and free world.' This kind of statement would not be surprising in the mouth of certain German expressionists, and in fact no other French painter except Rouault is as expressionist as Vlaminck. Was it his Flemish ancestry that made him surrender so willingly to these Teutonic tendencies? Perhaps so. In any case, a natural propensity made Vlaminck the most violent and extreme of the fauves; and, if fauvism were simply vehemence, he would be its most characteristic exponent, the symbol of fauvism.

58
Vlaminck
BATEAUX–LAVOIRS
1905

59
Vlaminck
PORTRAIT OF
DERAIN 1905

60
Derain
BALL AT SURESNES
1903

André Derain Although at the beginning of the century Vlaminck and Derain met regularly at Chatou, the two men had little in common. Whilst Vlaminck was in many respects self-taught, Derain had had a secondary education and had studied for entry to the Ecole Polytechnique in order to become an engineer. Having found his true vocation, he went to the Académie Carrière, where he met Matisse, as we have already seen. Never did he feel impelled to obey his instincts alone, to reject the contributions of academic teaching and of traditions. As he told Georges Duthuit: 'At eighteen, I was acquainted with every work of art it was possible to know through reproductions. What does one gain by lacking cul-

73

tural knowledge ?' Nothing, as we have seen, could be more opposed to Vlaminck's ideas. But around 1900 the two friends were less concerned with points on which they disagreed than with beliefs which brought them together.

In 1901 Derain made a copy of Ghirlandajo's *Christ Carrying the Cross,* in the Louvre, which succeeded in shocking the museum attendants. Then, before he had time to do very much more, he was called up for military service. His service lasted from 1901 to 1903 and, judging from the letters he sent to Vlaminck, it was a depressing time for him, 'atrocious, unbearable'—'I shall have aged

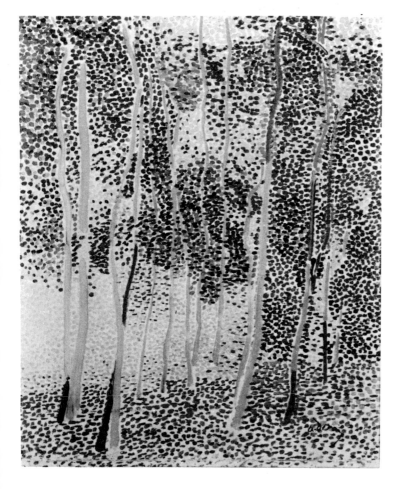

61
Derain
TREES
c. 1903

62 Derain The Bridge at Le Pecq 1904

a good deal by the time I come back,' he wrote, 'and I shall be pretty worn down and even more sceptical than before... sceptical about anarchy, about socialism, about philanthropy.' However, it was painting that preoccupied him first and foremost: 'Tell me if you have seen any new Van Goghs or Cézannes or anything.' 'As for painting,' he goes on to say, 'I am aware that the realist period has finished. We have only just begun as far as painting is concerned.' And on another occasion: 'A thing which bothers me is draughtsmanship. I would like to study kids' drawings. That's where the truth lies, without a doubt.' In the meantime he did drawings somewhat reminiscent of Toulouse-Lautrec for reviews like *Le Rire* and *Le Sourire,* as well as illustrating two of Vlaminck's books *(D'un Lit dans l'autre* and *Tout pour ça).* But in one of his letters he commented: 'People seem to think my drawings are like Lautrec's. That I find surprising...' In 1902 he declared: 'I am growing more and more discontented with drawing, which is a literary art form... our way certainly doesn't lie in that direction.' And the following year he stated that 'the great mistake all painters have made is to try to translate a momentary effect in nature, instead of realizing that a simple arrangement of light and shade would put one in the same frame of mind as a landscape which one had seen'. Here we have a principle which might well have been enunciated by a partisan of complete abstraction. If Derain did not go so far as this, he doubtless bore it in mind later and used it as a justification for the freedom with which he invented colours.

But when did he go back to painting? 'I am doing paintings of officers,' he wrote in 1903. 'It's a frightful trial. What a lot of trouble to take over rubbish! As far as my painting is concerned, I think too much and too carefully about it. I can envisage it too clearly. I can see my form. This is what is killing me, I try to immobilize my will between two known forms. That's total disaster.' A few days before being demobilized, he seemed more confident, saying that there was within himself 'on the whole not very much joy, but a great deal of determination, I think. And the determined effort to throw out of the window all nonsense, all near-misses and all indeci-

63
Derain
SNOW LANDSCAPE
AT CHATOU
1904-5

64 Derain L'Age d'Or 1905

sion.' Did he paint his *Ball at Suresnes* of 1903 *(Pl. 60)*, depicting soldiers, before or after he left the army? In any case, neither in colour nor in form does this canvas set out to be revolutionary. The colours are discreetly controlled by a draughtsmanship which, notwithstanding a few simplifications, follows an academic formula.

Derain's first move towards liberating himself from traditional teaching was to drown the form in coloured dots *(Trees, c.* 1903, *Pl. 61)*. It was doubtless the example of the neo-impressionists which suggested this solution to him, but he did not have recourse to it for long, in spite of the fact that it corresponded to the 'simple distribution of light and shade' which we heard him speak about to Vlaminck. He abandoned this pointillism probably because he considered the resulting picture too lacking in cohesion. Thus, a

65 Derain MOUNTAINS AT COLLIOURE 1905

little while later, we see him doing a large *Still-life* (private collection, Paris), with a flask, a bottle, some pieces of crockery and other
things arranged with a folded tablecloth on a table. The draughtsmanship here is clearly defined, the form synthetic and the colour put
on in flat tints. All this, as well as the dominant tones (somewhat
muted blues and reds) show that he has taken Gauguin as his example. The same influence, even down to the artist's facial features, can
be seen in his *Self-Portrait* of 1904 *(Pl. 69)*. Looking at landscapes
like *The Bridge at Le Pecq (Pl. 62)* or *The Bridge at Chatou* (private
collection, Paris) one is constantly aware of his desire to give a
sense of cohesion to details as well as to the whole: he divides the
picture somewhat arbitrarily into different fields of colour, cutting
down the detail of his figures to such an extent that they become
mere sketchy silhouettes, giving a jerky air to human and animal
movements. At the same time, he increases the vibrancy of his
colours, broadening and emphasizing his brushstrokes. And it is at

66 Derain CÔTE D'AZUR, NEAR AGAY 1905-6

this juncture that he is most like Vlaminck. But a simple comparison of his *Barges (Pl. 68)* with a similar work by his friend shows clearly how much the two artists differ from each other. Where Vlaminck is harsh, violent and passionate, Derain is polished and pleasing to the eye. Where Vlaminck is endowed with a sturdy strength which can be somewhat brutal and gross, Derain applies his colours with a lighter hand, making the brush describe an undulating movement— he retains some charm even in his daring innovations. Furthermore, Derain's painting is never highly-charged emotionally; it always retains a certain sweetness and grace, even a certain prettiness.

These qualities are even more noticeable in the paintings of the following year, 1905, when Derain worked at Collioure *(Pl. 65)* side by side with Matisse, who gave him encouragement and with whom, in the final analysis, he must always have felt a greater affinity than with Vlaminck. The dazzling light of the south inspired him to paint sunlit, gay and serene works. His palette becomes sweeter as he places delicate and vivid tones often side by side: oranges, pinks, violets partially replacing reds, with blues and emerald greens adding a restful freshness. Once more the brushstrokes spread further apart, especially when Derain is painting the sea. The white of the canvas then becomes a fluid element in which the different tints, put on in small rectangular strokes, seem to swim. Although the draughts-manship remains simplified and economical, it is more skilful than before. Contours (which are so rare and so blurred in Vlaminck) become more elegant and better defined. Having noticed, as he says in one of his letters, that in the Midi 'the light is very strong, the shadows very pale,' that 'shadow is a world of light and luminosity contrasting with the light of the sun,' Derain imparts a golden, airy, light colouring to certain of his works, such as *Collioure Harbour (Pl. 78)* which gives them a serene and happy atmosphere.

He did not confine himself to painting landscapes in 1905. He did two portraits in particular; of Vlaminck at Chatou and of Matisse at Collioure. Since he himself was painted by his two friends, it is highly relevant to compare these works, because each one manifests the artist's tendencies much more than the character of the model. In other words, whilst looking at the face he is painting, what each artist produces is a self-portrait. Doubtless in the way he drew the head of Vlaminck *(Pl. 67)* with, oddly enough, a black bowler hat on top of a pink face and orange hair, Derain was hinting at the violent, brusque, determined nature of the sitter, but there is a restraint in the colouring and certain refinements which are peculiar to the artist, reflecting his individual sensitivity, the pleasing aspects of which are also revealed in his *Portrait of Matisse (Pl. 72)*. It is illuminating to compare Derain's *Portrait of Matisse* with the *Self-Portrait (Pl. 71)* which Matisse painted in 1906, depicting himself as austere, determined, sure of his mission. One is tempted to say that he makes himself look less like an artist than an intransigent monk possessed by a grave, almost sombre passion. In Derain's version, on the other hand, the expression is not lacking in good humour, the gaze is not too penetrating. The beard, dark brown in Matisse's own picture, is brightened up with red and ochre tones. Elsewhere too the colouring aims to give an effect of cheerfulness; indeed, it narrowly misses being flashy (a yellow pipe-bowl standing out against a blue and mauve shirt). On the other hand, the head

67
Derain
PORTRAIT OF
VLAMINCK
1905

68
Derain
BARGES
1904

69
Derain
SELF–PORTRAIT
1904

70
Matisse
PORTRAIT OF DERAIN
1905

71
Matisse
SELF–PORTRAIT
1906

72
Derain
PORTRAIT OF MATISSE
1905

73 Derain SUNSET IN LONDON 1905

and bust are admittedly solidly constructed with broad and firm strokes. The draughtsmanship is more authoritative and the palette appreciably richer than in the same artist's *Portrait of Vlaminck*.

That this richness is due to his association with Matisse becomes clear on looking at the latter's *Portrait of Derain (Pl. 70)*. The colouring is thinned, distilled, the handling shows the lightest touch, daring and freer than Derain's, who in this work looks like a sort of highbrow artisan; his features are delicate, his expression thoughtful and a trifle worried. In Vlaminck's portrait, on the other hand, Derain has a somewhat plebeian and untidy air *(Pl. 59)*. Here a vehement red covers most of his face, while a wide dark line more or less outlines his chin and left cheek. The planes, clearly suggested by Matisse, are scarcely indicated here. Everything is heavy, crude

74 Derain BRIDGE OVER THE THAMES 1906

and aggressive. In short, everywhere Vlaminck's violent temperament is manifest.

In 1905, a stay in London led Derain to paint canvases such as
Sunset in London (Pl. 73), *The Houses of Parliament (Pl. 75)* and *Effects
of Sun on Water (Pl. 79)*, which display a different colouring from
the Collioure works. Here, cold tones, blues and greens predominate, and the artist gives to his canvases an iridescence which borders on preciosity. One year previously, Monet had also painted
The Houses of Parliament (Pl. 76) taking it from the same angle, but
a little nearer. In his work the sun, which can scarcely penetrate a
fog, forms an iridescent haze spread over the Thames; the forms are
completely blurred—the buildings seem more like a mirage than
tangible objects. If Derain too sets out to evoke the misty atmosphere

75
Derain
THE HOUSES OF
PARLIAMENT
1905

76
Monet
THE HOUSES OF
PARLIAMENT 1904

of the English capital, he is nonetheless at pains not to dissolve the objects, not to give them the hazy quality of evanescent ghosts. By the same token, although his brushstrokes become more densely packed, he does not let them dissolve into each other.

However, constantly anxious and scrupulous as he was, Derain soon tired of this broken touch and these forms lightly blurred by the mist. While at Collioure, he had already written to Vlaminck: 'If one doesn't make decorative patterns of colour, the only remaining task is to purify more and more the transposition of nature. But up to now we have only dealt with colouring. There is a parallel problem in draughtsmanship.' In 1906 he tried to concentrate on draughtsmanship. In a landscape in the Kunstmuseum, Basle, *Vineyards in Spring*, the trees and grasses serve as pretext for him to indulge in a complex, undulating and brilliant pattern of lines *(Pl. 82)*. In his *London Bridge (Pl. 77)* painted during a further stay in London in the spring of 1906, the line becomes heavier. He outlines objects vigorously and works hard to strengthen the overall stability. The colouring, too, becomes stronger. Gone is the flicker-

77 Derain LONDON BRIDGE 1906

78 Derain COLLIOURE 1905

79 Derain EFFECTS OF SUN ON WATER 1905

81 Derain POOL OF LONDON 1906

ing light seen in the London works of 1905. All the impressionist
elements which these works retained have disappeared: objects are
arrayed in pure and unmodelled colours with which we enter into
direct contact. We have the same impression when the atmospheric
veils become more apparent, as in the case of the *Pool of London*
(Pl. 81) or the *Bridge over the Thames (Pl. 74)*. However, nowhere is
the purity and freedom of the colour composition greater than in
Westminster Bridge (private collection, Paris) and *Hyde Park (Pl. 153)*.
Was it purely and simply a renewed influence of Gauguin that led
Derain to stray further from nature than he had done previously,
making decorative effect his primary concern ? The complete flatten-
ing out of the form, the eloquence which he manages to give to the
silhouettes, tempt one to think that he has also been influenced by
Japanese prints and Toulouse-Lautrec's posters. The *Woman in*
Chemise (Pl. 80), painted on his return to London, gives one the
same impression.) However that may be, he is extremely free in his
choice of colours as well as in their arrangement: he paints the paths
in the park pink, the street green, the sky and the river yellow, the

parapet and the pillars of the bridge blue, the pavement and the foliage on the trees red. And we must point out that his motives are of a strictly pictorial and not a symbolic order. His sole aim is to glorify colour, to paint pictures where it reigns supreme, where it is proudly and almost insolently triumphant. To this end, he spreads out the different shades in large zones; their limits, often curved, he sometimes outlines, adding a few quick, accurate, racy accents suggesting people walking, animals, vehicles. His search for vividness does not prevent him from trying to impose an order on these pictures, but the contrived element in them tends to be obscured by the playfulness with which they are painted.

Are there any other landscapes where fauvism has found a more convincing expression than this? There can be few in which high spirits have so well come to terms with the rules, in which spontaneous impulses so elegantly agree to be kept in check by the intellect.

82 Derain VINEYARDS IN SPRING 1906

83 Marquet Travelling Fair at Le Havre 1906

Albert Marquet There would be little reason for including Albert
Marquet among the fauves if fauvism were vivid colour and nothing
else, for indeed vivid colour has little place in this painter's work.
According to Matisse, his friend used grey in his pictures because
'he didn't have the wherewithal to buy colours, especially cad-
miums, which were expensive'. But Marquet himself has given
the lie to this explanation. 'I have only ever painted [with pure
tones] at Arcueil and in the Jardin du Luxembourg.' This was
in about 1898; he adds: 'It has happened that I have begun a canvas
in a brilliant tonality, going on to finish it in a grey notation. A
painting of a *Nude in a Studio,* known as the *Fauve Nude (Pl. 86)*
confirms that in 1898 Marquet did not reject pure tints. Like his
friend Matisse who, as we have seen, treated a similar subject in the
same year, his handling in places clearly demonstrates a neo-impressionist influence. The background is stippled with dots, patches

84 Marquet PONT-NEUF 1906

85 Marquet BEACH AT SAINTE-ADRESSE 1906

and streaks of red, green, blue and yellow, but the nude stands out
much more definitely than in Matisse's work, because the relief,
the volumes are accentuated by a systematic use of *chiaroscuro*. That
the *chiaroscuro* is based on the contrast of yellow and orange ochre
does not alter the fact that this is a traditional technique rejected by
Matisse and categorically impugned by fauvism. The conclusion
one must draw is that, in spite of his patches of bright colour,
Marquet is less daring than his friend, less inclined to break with
old habits.

Another of his canvases of 1904-5, *Matisse Painting a Nude in*

94

Manguin's Studio (Pl. 93) lends weight to this statement. Here again we can compare the two artists, because, as I have said, there is in the same museum a *Marquet Painting a Nude* by Matisse *(Pl. 92)*. Once again, Marquet uses stippling only in the background. The colouring, as much as the handling and the draughtsmanship, distinguishes the nude from the surroundings. The figure is defined by a contour, whilst in Matisse's work the outlines are not firmly defined and the patches of colour are scattered freely over the whole surface of the picture, so that they conceal the forms, rather as if they were snow flakes dancing in the air. As a result, Marquet's

88
Marquet
SERGEANT OF
THE COLONIAL ARMY
1907

89
Camoin
PORTRAIT OF
MARQUET
c. 1905

90
Marquet
Portrait of
André Rouveyre
1904

91
Marquet
Sergeant of
the Colonial Army
1907

picture is more easily deciphered at first glance than his friend's, and by more easily deciphered we mean more realistic, more traditionalist.

It is true that between these two works Marquet painted a *Portrait of Mme Matisse* in 1901 *(Pl. 87)*, where the colour is more vivid and more autonomous. One is even surprised by these oranges, pinks and mauves, vibrating somewhat restlessly next to blues and greens. Indeed, little is discernible in this portrait of Marquet's personality as it was to reveal itself a few years later. Here the painter takes up a position similar to the *nabis*, especially Vuillard, whom he

resembles in the intimacy of the scene, as well as his manner of applying the colours in little irregular strokes.

Marquet reveals quite a different manner in his *Portrait of André Rouveyre* of 1904 *(Pl. 90)*, and here it is his own personal style. No more pink or orange zones; a large patch of black, Rouveyre's outline, fills the centre of the canvas, standing out against a greyish background. Thus at the very time when his colleagues were extolling the colours of the spectrum, Marquet, who always made a habit of adopting contrary opinions, gave more importance to black; a black of a vibrancy, not to say a brilliance, which is remark-

94 Marquet APSE OF NOTRE-DAME 1902

able. And although this is merely a flat tint, we have the impression of seeing the model's body three-dimensionally, so meaningful are the contours. The means used to suggest distance, too, are elementary and at the same time highly expressive. In this respect, the picture has something of Manet's *The Fifer* (Musée du Louvre, Paris). An odd detail: the artist of *The Fifer* and that of the *Portrait of Rouveyre* both signed their pictures diagonally, the former on the lower right and the latter on the lower left; and in both cases with the obvious aim—and effect—of leading one's gaze into the background. However, even if Marquet here reminds one of Manet, we must acknowledge that he has created an original work. By painting three coloured bands across the canvas from right to left, representing a border running round the bottom of a partition behind Rouveyre, he indicates distance more precisely than did his predecessor. Then again, his handling is more terse and authoritative, less 'well-groomed' and more direct. His transposition is freer. The *Sergeant of the Colonial Army (Pl. 88)* bears the same characteristics, except that there is a greater range and vivacity in the colours, and that the distance is suggested by an even simpler technique : the figure is placed at a slight angle.

But Marquet was first and foremost a landscape painter and it is here that he found himself first. His *Apse of Notre-Dame* of 1902 *(Pl. 94)* already possesses most of the traits which subsequently came to characterize his pictures: the view taken from above; the vast perspective; long, swift diagonal lines accentuating depth; supple horizontal lines enclosing the composition and preventing the gaze from getting lost in an indefinite background; compact

95
Marquet
QUAI DES
GRANDS-AUGUSTINS
1905

96 Marquet BEACH AT FÉCAMP 1906

form; the disposition and form of objects summarily but accurately indicated; muted colours delicately graduated within the areas they occupy.

Marquet did other landscapes on the Normandy coast: for instance in 1906 he took as his subject the *Beach at Sainte-Adresse (Pl. 85)*, the *Beach at Fécamp (Pl. 96)* and the *Fourteenth July in Le Havre (Pl. 97)*. In the same year, brightly-coloured *Hoardings at Trouville,* together with red-striped bathing tents, inspired one of his most colourful and successful pictures *(Pl. 117)*. Moreover, some of his landscapes done between 1904 and 1907 are among the most accomplished works of the fauve period. They are certainly not very important pictures from an historical point of view; they are a far cry from the ambitious and fruitful experiments of Matisse, and they contributed only in a small degree to the elaboration of a new manner of painting; but they attract and hold one's attention by virtue of their very simplicity, their vibrancy, their distinctiveness and their solidity. If Marquet paints beaches, ports or quaysides *(Quai des Grands Augustins, Pl. 95)*, or the bridges over the Seine in Paris *(Pont-Neuf, Pl. 84)*, it is because he has a fondness for places where humanity lends animation to the impassivity of nature: an animation which he contemplates with an amused, ironical and mischievous eye. Since as a rule he looks at life from above, his human beings become diminutive and are shown at an angle which stresses any unusual or grotesque quality they might

97
Marquet
FOURTEENTH JULY
IN LE HAVRE
1906

98 Marquet SUNSET AT SAINTE-ADRESSE 1906

99
Marquet
SEATED NUDE

have. When he introduces them into his pictures, Marquet does not give much attention to details, keeping only the essential trait, the profile, an attitude, a movement. A simple patch or two simple strokes seemingly placed at random are enough to introduce a living being whose social position, character and future destiny we feel we can guess at. In other words, Marquet was an exceptional draughtsman: a gift which he reveals in his brush drawings more than in his paintings *(Pls. 99–104)*. With equal skill, he captures on the paper the dawdling schoolgirl and the old wife holding a baby on her knees, cab horses resting or galloping, the determined stride of the businessman and the tiny steps of the old maid. His line, usually broad and thick, has a lively movement, one might say a certain whimsy too, were it not so powerfully evocative. It is, in fact, selective in the extreme, possessing a concision which has led to its being compared to Hokusai's line, although it is more expansive

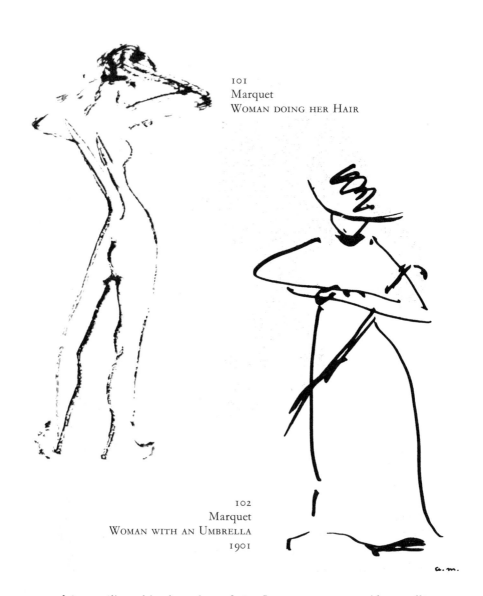

101
Marquet
WOMAN DOING HER HAIR

102
Marquet
WOMAN WITH AN UMBRELLA
1901

and less calligraphic than that of the Japanese master. Above all,
Marquet's line has a more carefree movement, constantly revealing
his own peculiar dry humour; his form and his composition constantly reveal qualities of daring which, in spite of the delicate restraint
of his colour harmonies, earn him a place of his own in the fauvist
movement.

103
Marquet
MAN FROM BEHIND
1901

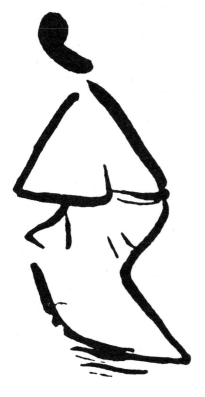

104
Marquet
JAPANESE WOMAN
1901

Charles Camoin, Henri Manguin, Maurice Marinot, Jean Puy, Louis Valtat   Although the special page of *L'Illustration* of 4 November 1905 reproduced works by Manguin, Puy and Valtat, these three artists, like Camoin and Marinot, are distinguished primarily by their moderation: they are reformers rather than revolutionaries.   Certainly they too were reacting against impressionism; their aim was to restore solidity to objects and a sense of construction to the picture; they liked colour to be pure and occasionally vivid.   But in spite of all this, they remained much closer to visible reality than the other fauves, and by that very fact much more traditionalist.   Little given to theorizing, seeking above all to express their pleasure in living, they continued in the last resort to respect the essential principles of naturalism. Instead of trying to transcribe forms in a new spirit, they were usually content to simplify them by means of stylizations.

Valtat, the oldest amongst them, was using a vivid palette as far back as 1892-4. He was as close to the neo-impressionists as to Gauguin, in that his colour was at times applied in little patches and at times spread out in flat tints *(Nude in the Garden,* Dr Jean Valtat collection, Paris). Pure tones remain in the *Water Carriers at Arcachon* of 1894 *(Pl. 106)* and in the *Promenade on the Champs-Elysées* of 1898 *(Pl. 107),* but the draughtsmanship is different from that of his earlier works; its complacent inflexions are reminiscent of the *nabis* or the floral manner of *Art Nouveau.* Little wriggling strokes reappear in the *Fishergirl* of 1902, whilst the *Seine and Eiffel Tower* of 1904 *(Pl. 111)* hark back once more to neo-impressionism. Broadened, heavily-emphasized patches crowd in, one might almost

106 Valtat WATER CARRIERS AT ARCACHON 1897

say pile up on each other. Of course, Valtat's aim is not simply to interpret light; colour has an intrinsic importance in his work and his colour harmonies are occasionally daring. However, one would not think of ranking him with Marquet or Vlaminck, let alone with Derain or Matisse. This is because his vision is rarely anything other than traditionalist, because his painting is often unconvincing. Valtat serves to demonstrate that pure tints or a broad handling and a simplified form are not enough to create a new style of painting.

This is also true of Camoin and Manguin, Puy and Marinot. Of course, this does not mean that these artists have not given us pictures which hold our attention. Camoin in particular painted in about 1905 a *Portrait of Marquet (Pl. 89)* which is a most attractive work. The face is that of a man who seems to be clinging to a personal obsession in order to keep awake; but beneath the apparent indifference one can detect the inquisitive and quizzical observer in

107 Valtat PROMENADE ON THE CHAMPS-ÉLYSÉES 1898

108
Manguin
PORTRAIT OF
JEAN PUY
1906

Marquet. The style of this work is by no means lacking in originality. The white of the canvas, still visible around the eyes and the mouth, constitutes a sort of negative draughtsmanship. The whole painting has the quality of a first sketch, which intensifies the impression that the model has been seized in the attitude and expression of a moment, but a moment which reveals something fundamental. The colour avoids any kind of violence, but the line is firm and decisive. The forms are rendered in a geometrical way, and the contrasts between curves and straight lines, segments of the circle and triangles, betray the influence of Cézanne, with whom Camoin was in sympathy and whose advice he had put to good use without imitating his pictures.

Manguin has left us a *Portrait of Jean Puy (Pl. 108)*, which, in a

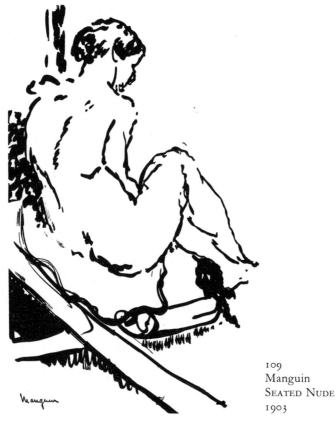

109
Manguin
SEATED NUDE
1903

way, is more fauve in character than the *Portrait of Marquet* in that
its colouring is more resonant: the wide red surface of a pullover
occupies a quarter of the canvas, contrasting with cold tints distributed over the trousers, and the background, whilst the face presents
delicate tones. The drawing is more supple and more flowing than
Camoin's, although not more expressive: in fact it displays markedly
less inventiveness. Generally speaking, invention plays a minor
part in Manguin's work, whether his subject is a nude, a still–life or
a landscape like the *Fourteenth July at Saint–Tropez* of 1905 *(Pl. 110)*.
And if certain of his colours can be extremely vivid and easy on
the eye, the whole hardly presents a striking revelation; neither in
his handling of form nor space does Manguin renew our traditional
concept of nature.

110
Manguin
FOURTEENTH JULY
AT SAINT-TROPEZ
1905

111
Valtat
SEINE AND
EIFFEL TOWER
1904

112
Dufy
<small>SELF-PORTRAIT</small>
1898

Raoul Dufy   Dufy came to Paris in 1900. Although he studied in the same studio at the Ecole des Beaux-Arts as his friend and colleague Friesz, unlike him he did not often go to the Louvre: the only keen admiration he felt was for Claude Lorrain. But, on the other hand, he did often stop in the rue Laffitte to look at the impressionists in the windows of the Durand-Ruel Gallery and the Cézannes and Gauguins displayed by Vollard. It was these artists, too, especially Monet, Pissarro and Degas, who influenced his development. Between 1900 and 1904, he liked to paint the teeming life of the Parisian streets and the Normandy coastal resorts with a light palette dominated by a grey-blue, producing works which have something of the delicacy of his predecessor from Le Havre, Eugène Boudin. But he eventually realized that by working in the impressionist manner he was leaving himself 'out of the picture'. And, as he later confided to Pierre Courthion, one day at Sainte-Adresse, looking at his tubes of colour and his brushes, he asked himself: 'How, with what I have here, can I succeed in rendering,

not what I see, but what is, what has an existence for me, *my reality ?...*
I then set to work drawing, taking from nature what suited my
needs. Then I drew the contours of each object in black mixed with
white, each time leaving in the middle the white of the paper which
I then coloured in with a specific and quite intense tone. What did
I have ? Blue, green, ochre, not many colours. However, the result
surprised me. I had discovered what it was I was really looking for.'
The sight of Matisse's *Luxe, Calme et Volupté* at the Salon des Indépendants of 1905 encouraged him to venture further in this direction. 'On looking at that picture,' he declared in 1925, 'I grasped
all the new reasons for painting; the realism of the impressionists
lost its charm for me as I contemplated the miracle of the imagination introduced into draughtsmanship and colour.'

113 Dufy RIGGED YACHT 1904

Does this mean that he drew closer to Matisse ? For the moment, he had more in common with Marquet, with whom he became friends, in whose company he painted at Fécamp in 1904, and at Trouville and Le Havre in 1906. So there is nothing surprising in the fact that he too painted *Hoardings at Trouville (Pl. 118)*. Nor is it at all surprising that he too drew his inspiration for his *Fourteenth July* from a street in Le Havre where the flags produced zones of sizzling reds *(Pl. 119)*. Nevertheless although Dufy and Marquet

114
Dufy
WINDOW WITH
COLOURED PANES
1906

115 Dufy OLD HOUSES AT HONFLEUR 1906

116
Dufy
SUNSHADES
1906

117 Marquet HOARDINGS AT TROUVILLE 1906

were not the first to depict such a subject—streets metamorphosed by the national holiday had also been painted by Manet, Monet and Van Gogh—their works are very different from those of their predecessors. Their flags are not, like those of Manet, patches of colour partly blurred by the atmosphere; nor are they the teeming multitude of colours which Monet needed to express his crowding impressions; nor are they the red and blue gashes in whose violent collision Van Gogh expressed the turmoil of his soul; they are arrangements of pure colours unrestrainedly asserting themselves in all their unexpected solemnity against the lightly tinted grisaille of the houses.

Dufy, like Marquet, was interested in the sight of busy streets and seaside resorts, and he was fond of summing up in an outline the attitudes and movements of men and women observed from a distance. But his draughtsmanship is less sharply defined than Marquet's, whilst his colour is in general richer and more vivid. It is just this vividness of colouring, as well as the freedom of his conception, that distinguishes some of his works of 1906–7 which

118 Dufy HOARDINGS AT TROUVILLE 1906

take as their subject *Fourteenth July in Le Havre* (private collections, Paris). In his desire to emphasize the feeling of joy which he is trying to communicate, Dufy does not hesitate to enlarge the flags in the background out of all proportion, thus giving a more lyrical quality to the red–white–and–blue which is the main 'hero' of the picture. In the *Sunshades* of 1906 *(Pl. 116)* he once again ventures to put a large red patch in the middle of the canvas, in this way heralding the sly and delectable audacities which he was subsequently to practise with such unconcern.

For the rest, it would not be true to say that his vision was always original. In more than one instance one can spot the naturalistic formula below his simplified surface. And it is sufficient to compare his *Window with Coloured Panes (Pl. 114)* with Matisse's *Open Window* to see how cautious his draughtsmanship can still be in 1906. Obviously, the regular quality of his form and his emphatic contours are explained by his need to make an absolute break with impressionism, whose memory must have haunted him all the more that he sometimes depicted subjects similar to those treated by Monet and

119 Dufy FOURTEENTH JULY AT LE HAVRE 1906

his friends. Furthermore, although straight lines are emphasized in the *Window*, as in *Old Houses at Honfleur (Pl. 115)*, elsewhere, in the *Bal champêtre at Falaise* of 1906 for instance (Mme Bourdon collection, Paris), curves are predominant. They have a laconic quality, indicating that Dufy was looking for a form which diverged from realism, into which he could infuse the imagination whose value had become manifest to him on looking at *Luxe, Calme et Volupté*. He displays the same concern more clearly when, in about 1907, he painted *Jeanne with Flowers (Pl. 125)*. The colour, the draughtsmanship, the composition, everything here indicates that

120
Dufy
LE HAVRE HARBOUR
c. 1906

121
Dufy
THE BEACH AT
SAINTE-ADRESSE
1906

122 Dufy EFFECTS OF SUN, SAINTE-ADRESSE 1906

123
Dufy
THE APÉRITIF
1908

124 Dufy ANGLERS *c.* 1908

his aim is a decorative arrangement, similar to the one he admired in Matisse. However, this led him to give a regularity to form which he did not care for in the long run: thus he was soon to be in violent reaction against it. In the *Anglers* of *c.* 1908 *(Pl. 124),* the lines are harsh; the human beings walking about on the beach have the stiff and jerking movements of marionettes; not only has the composition ceased to be static, it has lost the harmonious quality of the earlier work. Dufy is even wider of his mark than before, since nothing is further from his nature than violence and roughness (although he does seem to turn to it as one has recourse to a remedy). A greater sense of ease becomes apparent in his *Lady in Pink* of 1907-8 *(Pl. 126):* here the line, although synthetic and heavily stressed in parts, does not lack suppleness; suggesting even at this

126
Dufy
LADY IN PINK
1907–8

point the light and apparently free and easy air peculiar to Dufy once he had acquired a truly personal manner.

Meanwhile he continued to feel his way. In *The Apéritif* of 1908 *(Pl. 123)*, one sees the reappearance of curves similar to those in the *Bal Champêtre at Falaise*. However, Dufy was now drawing further away from the external world: the relationships between the figures and their exact situation in space is less important here than the relationships between the greens and the pinks, between the lines which inflect and sway as they describe 'abstract' rhythms. And yet it took him a further ten years to become the draughtsman of powerfully evocative abbreviations and the sparkling colourist, rapid, graceful and charming, whom we all know and to whom we shall return later.

127
Friesz
PORTRAIT OF
FERNAND FLEURET
1907

Émile-Othon Friesz Of the three fauves who were natives of Le Havre, Friesz was the first to arrive in Paris. In 1898 he entered the Ecole des Beaux-Arts, but it was less Bonnat's teaching than his visits to the Louvre which helped him to find his way. There he made copies of Veronese, Rubens, Delacroix: in other words, he already manifested a preference for baroque movement and grouping. Having met Pissarro and Guillaumin in 1901, he drew closer to impressionism, which he had doubtless already encountered in Le Havre. Indeed, it was at Le Havre and Honfleur that the young Monet, Jongkind and Boudin had painted; and some of Boudin's works could be studied in the municipal art gallery.

In about 1904, Friesz, who had met Matisse, felt the need, as he put it, 'to escape from the mediocrity of direct emotion'. Whilst acknowledging his debt to the impressionists, he realized that 'they did not construct their pictures, which were mere active documentations of nature: arrangements, not compositions.' It then seemed to him that colour was to be a 'means of salvation,' and 'the study of complementary and contrasting colours' led him to 'this conception, to render the light of the sun by a technique composed of coloured orchestrations—passionate transpositions (with nature as their starting point)...' Visits to the Midi hastened his emancipation: he worked at Cassis in 1904 and La Ciotat in 1905. However, while he used primary colours, he did not strive after brilliant harmonies. Pale pinkish tints, and not reds, are dominant in his works. His form, too, is less emancipated from traditional teaching than that of Matisse or Derain, although his line, with its emphasis on curves, does not lack passion. The most interesting thing about some of his pictures, and especially the little *Landscape* of the Musée National d'Art Moderne in Paris, is doubtless his notation of space: no lines receding towards the horizon, but planes spaced out, differentiated by colour. Owing to the distribution of warm and cold tones, the lack of cohesion of these planes is only dimly felt, and at first sight the picture has a somewhat flat quality.

In 1906, Friesz, who, like Matisse had set up his studio in the former Oiseaux convent, spent some time in Antwerp in the company of Braque. Following the demands of the subject, the canvases he painted in the harbour have a more muted colour composition *(Pl. 128)*. The following year, he painted a fine portrait of *Fernand Fleuret* in his room *(Pl. 127)* sitting by a table holding a book. The poet, who is seen from above, is raising his head as though someone had suddenly come into the room. His mind seems full of what he has just been reading; one guesses that the outside world has little reality for him. In other words, the picture is like a snapshot, although it is carefully composed. During the same year Friesz painted more landscapes at La Ciotat; and it is in these works that his art attains its highest degree of rapture. Not that the colours in these works are brighter than in 1905, but they are more pure and luminous. In the reds and oranges of the landscape in the Pierre Lévy collection in Troyes, the gaiety and ardour, the calm and

128 Friesz Harbour at Antwerp 1906

129 Braque Harbour at Antwerp 1906

130 Friesz LANDSCAPE AT LA CIOTAT 1907

implacability of the broad sun of the Midi are admirably contained
(Pl. 130). The draughtsmanship too has matured: more alert and
more expressive, it has become a handwriting. The lines swell out
or grow thinner, they are long impetuous curves or little tense
flourishes, always distinguished by their sturdy yet supple decisive-
ness. If Friesz proves here that he is a baroque artist, he shows at
the same time that he is not carried away by his lyricism to the point
of forgetting that a solid structure is indispensable to the picture.
Doubtless it was Cézanne's influence in the first instance which
prevented him from being guided solely by his temperament, but
he also profited from his study of Japanese prints, as his evocative
calligraphy and flattened forms demonstrate.

131 Braque The Landing-Stage, L'Estaque 1906

Georges Braque Braque's name is so intimately linked with cubism, it so immediately calls to mind a sober painting, rich in greys and browns, in greens and blacks, that one is at first surprised to hear it mensioned in connection with the fauvists. It is true that Braque's fauvism was of short duration, and is represented by only about twenty of his pictures.

Braque arrived in Paris in 1900 to work as a house-painter. He attended the Académie Humbert from 1902 to 1904. (He did not stay longer than two months in Bonnat's studio, where he renewed his acquaintance with Friesz and Dufy). He often went to the Louvre to admire the Egyptian and Greek sculptures as well as the Poussins and, more especially, the Corots. He also used to look at the impressionists at Durand-Ruel's or Vollard's. Although he was attracted by Renoir, Monet, Van Gogh and Seurat, Cézanne left him cold at first, and he positively disliked Degas and Gauguin. However, it was Matisse's and Derain's Collioure canvases at the Salon d'Au-

132 Braque L'ESTAQUE 1906

tomne of 1905 which led to his conversion to fauvism. The following summer, he accompanied Friesz to Antwerp and, as the latter was already working in the new manner, it was natural that Braque should be influenced by him. However, his *Harbour at Antwerp* *(Pl. 133)*, and the picture of the same subject in the National Gallery of Art in Ottawa *(Pl. 129)*, show his technique to be much less spontaneous and more carefully thought-out than Friesz's. In addition, his pictures contain purples, pinks, greenish blues, ochre yellows; in other words, his colouring is far from being crude.

In October 1906, he went and settled for several months in the south of France, at l'Estaque, where Cézanne had also spent some time. It was there that he painted *The Harbour* (Musée National d'Art Moderne, Paris) and *The Landing-Stage (Pl. 131)*, showing the sea bounded by the quayside, by houses, and by the landscape with mountains rising in the distance. Although water and sky occupy an important place in these works, other canvases (in particu-

133 Braque Harbour at Antwerp 1906

lar *L'Estaque* in the Aimé Maeght collection *(Pl. 132)* or the *House behind Trees (Pl. 134))* are almost completely taken up with solid objects: a plot of stony ground, hills, trees, a nearby house on which the gaze comes to rest. His palette has become more vivid: pink tones have partially given way to reds; blues and greens are more insistent and less cold. However, Braque never achieves the brilliance of Derain, or rather he does not seek it, preferring to retain a calm, velvety, intimate quality. His skies are clouded over (which is probably due to the time of year), his light is not dazzling. Braque's restraint is revealed not only in the nature of the colours he chooses but also in the manner in which he applies them to the canvas, using both patches and small rectangular strokes, the latter in particular being used to suggest the fluidity of the sky and sea. Derain, in the previous year, had also used small rectangular strokes, but his were vigorous and hurried, and as a rule short and relatively thin, nearly becoming dots in places; Braque's are fairly long, broad and some-

134 Braque HOUSE BEHIND TREES 1906

135
Braque
LA CIOTAT
1907

what hesitant. Furthermore, the white of the canvas showing through here and there does not make the paintings more radiant, serving only to sweeten the tones and to make the composition lighter, more open to the air.

Braque returned to the Midi during the summer of 1907 and spent some time at La Ciotat, where he was joined by Friesz. Once again, one has the impression that he came under the latter's influence: his strokes lengthen and start to look like arabesques. But he had already foretold this evolution in the earlier L'Estaque works, the *L'Estaque (Pl. 132),* for instance, where line already plays a prominent role, being used both in the definition of form and in the structure of the composition. Moreover, his lines do not become, like Friesz's, S-curves which move with the swift and smooth elegance of a greyhound. They form rows of arches encompassing objects in successive spans. Again, although Braque's colours become more definite, they still avoid all exuberance *(Landscape at La Ciotat,* D.-H. Kahnweiler collection, Paris) and lack the jubilant luminosity of Friesz's colouring. On the other hand, one does from time to time notice radical changes in Braque's representation of space: as in another *Landscape at La Ciotat (Pl. 137),* which is deliberately

136
Braque
La Ciotat
1907

134

137
Braque
La Ciotat
1907

constructed in height rather than in depth; so that while accepting
that the lie of the land suggested this solution, one is obliged to see
here a step towards the reduction of the third dimension, the 'flatten-
ing out' which was to characterize Braque's painting during the
following years. This tendency becomes much more marked in the
works inspired by L'Estaque which the artist was to paint a few
months later, not with the subject in front of him but in his studio
in Paris. Here the draughtsmanship becomes more disciplined; the
arches grow smaller, the lines stiffen, break off and join up again
angularly; the colouring grows muted. Braque was abandoning
fauvism and moving in the direction of another style.

138 Van Dongen WOMEN AT A BALUSTRADE 1910

139 Van Dongen ANITA 1905

Kees Van Dongen The story goes that Kees Van Dongen, a native
of Delfshafen near Rotterdam, arrived in Paris on 12 July 1897,
on an excursion train and with a return ticket. His (avowed) aim:
to be in the French capital for the 14 July celebrations. However,
although he could not understand a word of French, he threw
away his ticket and decided to stay in Paris to paint. His decision
was probably less sudden than the legend would have us believe:
he had doubtless already thought about it before boarding the
train in Rotterdam, since he had already been painting for some
years (landscapes, horses on the quayside, tarts in the port, sail-

141
Van Dongen
PORTRAIT OF
D. H. KAHNWEILER
1907

ors). His art was influenced by Van Gogh and it was probably
Van Gogh's example that prompted him to go and settle in Paris.
He had difficulty in scraping a living at first, working as a market
porter at the Halles, a furniture remover, a house-painter. He did
portraits on the terraces of cafés and submitted drawings to humo-
rous magazines such as *L'Assiette au Beurre,* to which Jacques
Villon and, later, Juan Gris also contributed. About 1905, he set up
in Montmartre in the famous *Bateau-Lavoir* in the rue Ravignan,
where he was a neighbour of Picasso. His development is no less
difficult to trace than Vlaminck's, for he too as a rule did not bother
to date his pictures.

Like almost all the other fauves, he went through an impressionist
phase at first, during which he did mostly landscapes inspired by
Normandy or Holland. But he also painted views of Paris, scenes
observed in the streets and cafés of Montmartre, and it is through

these works, where he showed himself receptive to the teaching of
Toulouse-Lautrec, Forain, Steinlen, that he found his own personal
manner. In *The Sideshow* of 1904-5 *(Pl. 140)*, the female dancer and
the barker who are doing their utmost to capture the interest of an
invisible audience, still have much in common with Lautrec's figures,
but one would look in vain for the latter's incisive draughtsmanship.
The form is frayed out and in places blurred by a shower of hatchings and tightly-packed strokes of colour reminiscent of impressionist technique. However, Van Dongen was not content simply

142
Van Dongen
LA BELLE FATHMA
AND HER TROUPE
1906

to paint effects of light; it was colour that absorbed his attention; and the precise object of those violent hatchings was to make it quiver with intensity. Did he realize that he scarcely achieved his aim? In any case, shortly afterwards he began to use flat tints and to animate the surfaces with more discreet strokes; and it was only then that his originality was revealed and that his fauve period really began (unlike that of the vast majority of his colleagues, it did not end in 1907 but lasted until about 1913).

His subjects? Cabaret dancers, circus clowns, women nude or dressed in floral frocks; an occasional portrait, that of the picture-dealer D.-H. Kahnweiler (1907) for instance *(Pl. 141)*; riders in the Bois de Boulogne, race courses, landscapes and picturesque scenes

143
Van Dongen
OLD CLOWN
c. 1906

140

which he came across on his travels in Morocco, Spain and Egypt.
Moreover, for the most part these subjects did not attract him
simply as subject matter for his painting, he found them interesting
in themselves. Van Dongen loved life perhaps even more than
painting; and life for him was life in the world, the sort that one
only meets by getting out into it. 'Does a man love life who spends
days patiently recording the colours and tones of an apple?' he
asks. 'Does the man understand life who only looks at nature
through the shutters of his room? Does the man experience life
who conjures up the mysteries of the Orient in his home?'

His motive for painting was less to resolve artistic problems
than to possess more fully the things which attracted him in reality.
He was little concerned about finding a new way of representing
distance; he was content to place his figures on a bare background

or to suggest a depth which remained indefinite *(La Belle Fathma and her Troupe,* 1906 *(Pl. 142).* Forms are simplified, but he avoids altering them too much, even for the sake of radically transposing them. It is only when he looks at figures and objects from a distance that he tries to give them an evocative air. On these occasions he gives to the walking figures bodies which are elongated and thinned down in the extreme; a seated woman becomes an S tipped over backwards; gipsies trotting by on their donkeys become silhouettes caught with a few brief cursive strokes.

But Van Dongen preferred to look at human figures from close to. His dancers and clowns stand in the foreground of the painting

145
Van Dongen
LIVERPOOL
NIGHT CLUB
1906

146
Van Dongen
WOMAN WITH JEWELS
1905

so that their presence immediately imposes itself; and usually it is simply a physical presence. Van Dongen's psychological interest is limited. Devoid of spiritual curiosity, he scarcely ever feels impelled to penetrate into the labyrinth of the soul; he never examines souls in the instant when their deepest, truest natures are revealed; in solitude. He only looks at the face which men and women put on before the world, before others. There is no denying that his *Old Clown c.* 1906 *(Pl. 143)* shows us an emaciated face, bearing the harsh marks of age and weariness, but such a face is an exception. In any case, how could we linger long over it when our attention is distracted by the other elements of the picture: the splendour of the colouring, the orange of the hair, the pale blue of the shadow on his chin, the red and white checks of the costume, the subtleties of the greys in the shirt? However, it is when he takes the nude, or the head and shoulders of a woman, as his subject that Van Dongen most clearly reveals the importance he attaches to the physical element, to everything that appeals to one's sensuality. He leaves no room for doubt that he is above all a sensual man, eager and even impatient to go beyond the pleasures of sight, and to take the bodies of women in his arms. For him a nude is not an arrangement of forms, a coloured architecture, as it is for Matisse, it is soft and warm, something that he wants to caress even while he is painting it. In other words, whilst for Matisse sensuality is strictly limited to its role in the painting—as is proved by his *Gipsy* not less than his *Blue Nude*—everything in Van Dongen's work incites us to see the unclothed body and to think of the sensual rapture to which it can give rise in reality (*Anita, Pl. 139*).

147
Van Dongen
PORTRAIT OF
FERNANDE OLIVIER
1907–8

For the rest, almost all the women he depicts seem to have only one concern: to exploit their charms, to attract, to seduce. Whether they are proudly displaying their breasts or hiding them beneath silk, or muslin, they like to crown their often opulent tresses with a huge hat which accentuates their worldly, bizarre quality. Here too one thinks of Matisse, and the role played by hair arrangement in his *Woman with Hat*; although it is in keeping with the fashion of the time, it is scarcely more than a complex of colours and forms. In Van Dongen, on the other hand, the hat acts first and foremost as an adornment or a means of revealing the face and nature of the wearer *(Pl. 144)*. His mission is to emphasize the *femme fatale* or the sphinx behind these painted faces; he has to give a headier or more brazen element to their seductiveness.

It is clear that colour has also an intrinsic value in Van Dongen's work. He is a rich and distinctive colourist, one of the most original among the fauves. By turns crude and delicate, pleasing and aggressive, he juxtaposes the piquant and the tender, the colour which borders on vulgarity and the one that holds our attention by its refinement. In his *Women at a Balustrade* of 1910 *(Pl. 138)*, a black hat sits on top of ultramarine hair; very red lips stand out in an ochre face with green shadows, while pink tones subtly vibrate in the dress. 'Painting', according to Van Dongen, 'is not nature, it is something essentially artificial'.

If he worked with reckless enthusiasm, if he did not always avoid giving the impression of carelessness in his works, he could also create marvels of distinction, the rarest and most delicious graduations of tones. His *Spanish Dancer, c.* 1912 *(Pl. 148)* displays such a vivacity and an accuracy of touch that it reminds one of Manet or Frans Hals or even Velazquez, so fine are his greys and pinks, his whites and pale blues, so broad and at the same time effective and precise is his technique.

After 1918, Van Dongen's painting was to lose some of its best qualities, when he became a society portrait-painter, the only one to emerge from *avant-garde* circles, portraying his sitters with not a little ferocity, notwithstanding his high reputation among his clients. But during his fauve period he was an artist full of vigour, richness and pungency not only in his colours but in his subject matter. If he was akin to Vlaminck in the importance he attached to direct expression, he was distinguished from him by a more sensitive eye, a more demanding taste and a more solidly-founded skill, and by the greater range of his technique.

The Contribution of Fauvism

The primary characteristic of the fauves—which almost all of them shared to a considerable degree—is their desire to increase the powers of colour. They were indeed indebted to others, to Van Gogh and Gauguin in particular, but the most advanced of the fauves went far beyond their forerunners; their colour is freer and more violent.

More violent? The fire which burned in Van Gogh's soul was fiercer, more all-consuming than that which burned in Vlaminck's, yet nonetheless the former often seems reserved in comparison with the latter; there is less vehemence (which does not mean that there is less energy) in his expression. In the last analysis, Van Gogh's aim was harmony. The fauves (and here I am referring to those who expressed themselves the most radically) prefer colours which make a violent and startling impact. Like their predecessors, the fauves use complementary colours; but the inter-play of colours is more complex, the relationships more tense, and there are subtle and strident dissonances. To be convinced of this, one has only to compare Van Gogh's *Portrait of the Artist with Severed Ear (Pl. 150)* with Matisse's *Portrait with Green Streak (Pl. 151)*. There are four zones of pure colour in the Van Gogh: two in the figure (the green of the jacket, the blue of the fur hat), two in the background (orange against the blue, red against the green). The face is flesh-coloured with streaks of orange and blue; the bandage and the shirt-collar are whitish. In the Matisse, on the other hand, there are only pure colours, and their number is considerably increased: besides vermilion, we see purple, pink, ochre, two blues and three greens. In addition, the colour composition is not elementary as it is in the Van Gogh; in one place only are the green and the red placed side by side. Elsewhere they are separated and can only 'signal to each other'. The orange which complements the blue is implicit rather

150
Van Gogh
PORTRAIT OF
THE ARTIST
WITH SEVERED EAR
1889

151
Matisse
PORTRAIT WITH
GREEN STREAK
1905

than explicit; it is suggested by the juxtaposition of ochre and vermilion. This is just one example of the freedom with which the fauves handled colour. Let us look at some others. In the *Gipsy*, Matisse represents shadows as red, pink, orange and green, disregarding principles established by the impressionists and respected by Van Gogh; his apparent aim is to prove that there is nothing absolute about these principles. Similarly Derain, when he painted *Three Figures in a Meadow (Pl. 152)*, sometimes showed shadows as red and sometimes as purple or blue.

Even more than their predecessors, the fauves conceive of the picture as a world apart; a world which does indeed remain in contact with visible reality, but which is not simply its reflection. Far from taking nature as its model, the fauve painter regards it simply as a point of departure. He is less interested in objects than in the sensation aroused by coming into contact with them; and this sensation affects not only his eye but the whole of his psyche. The fauves' main aim is to transcribe this sensation in its sharpest, most intense and therefore most subjective terms. Moreover, he effects this transcription in a particular idiom, that of pure colour, and this too carries fauve painting out of the realm of visual reality.

In 1908 Matisse wrote in his 'Notes d'un Peintre' ('a painter's notes') published by *La Grande Revue ;* 'If I scatter blue, green and red sensations on a white canvas, every successive stroke diminishes the importance of each of the preceding ones. I am to paint an interior: before me I have a cupboard which gives me a sensation of a really lively red, so I apply a red which gives me satisfaction. A relationship is established between this red and the white of the canvas. If next to it I place a green, if I interpret the floor by a yellow, this creates additional relationships between this yellow and the white of the canvas, which will give me satisfaction. But these different colours diminish each other. The different symbols I use must be balanced in such a way that they don't destroy each other completely. To do this I must order my ideas; the relationship between the colours must be established in such a way that it keeps them together and upholds them instead of destroying them. A new combination of colours will succeed the former and provide the colour composition for my picture. I have to transpose, and it is for this reason that people imagine that my picture has undergone

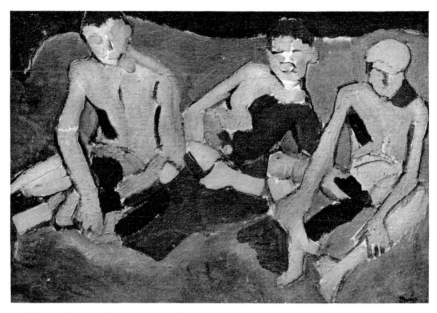

152 Derain THREE FIGURES IN A MEADOW 1906

a radical transformation when, after successive modifications, red has replaced green as the dominant colour. I am unable to make a servile copy of nature; nature must be interpreted and subjected to the spirit of the picture. When I have worked out all my tonal relationships, the result should be a living harmony of colours, comparable to that of a musical composition.'

After these explanations, which reveal the lucidity with which he used technical devices, Matisse stresses that 'the expressive quality of colours is communicated purely instinctively,' and that the paint-er's choice 'is not based on any scientific theory' but 'on observa-tion, on emotions, on sensitive experience.' In short, unlike Signac whose 'theoretical knowledge leads him to use this or that colour here or there,' Matisse 'is simply seeking to transpose his feelings into colours'. And he adds: 'There is an equilibrium indispensable to colour composition which may lead me to make formal modifica-tion to a figure or to transform my composition. I keep on working until I have established this equilibrium throughout the picture. Then comes the moment when all the parts have found their defini-

153 Derain HYDE PARK 1906

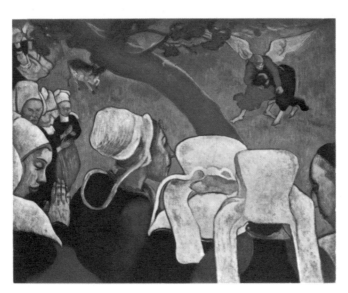

154
Gauguin
VISION AFTER
THE SERMON
1888

tive relationships; from that moment on it would be impossible for me to add any further touches without entirely recasting it.'

I think it is fair comment to say that such phrases would scarcely have surprised Van Gogh and Gauguin. It must be acknowledged, however, that in their work the links between art and nature were never as tenuous as they are in Matisse, and more particularly that they never placed so much emphasis on pure painting as did Matisse. This did not, however, prevent Matisse from declaring: 'My principal aim is to express myself... For me, expression does not reside in intense emotion as manifested in a facial expression or a violent gesture. Expression for me is the whole arrangement of my picture: the area occupied by the bodies, the spaces around them, the proportions, all this belongs to it. Composition is the art of making a decorative arrangement of elements from which the painter can choose to express his feelings.'

Another peculiarity of the fauves is their technique. In the beginning, at least, it was hasty, full of apparent clumsiness and carelessness, so that as a rule the picture looked like a sketch. This was deliberate; the expressive force of the painting was all the more direct in that one could still perceive in every colour the movements of the hand which had applied it. Nor is that all: this technique disturbs, perforates, dislocates the form of objects; and if objects are altered or diminished in importance, this is not as in an impressionist painting, for the benefit of light and atmosphere, but because they have become mere vehicles for sensory impressions, mere elements in a painting. Nevertheless, the fauves did not go so far as to take the picture to pieces, as the cubists were to do. Matisse, as we have seen, attempted to get back to a closed form, but his form reveals that it has been shaken to its foundations; it has lost its naturalistic character, been purified and synthesized.

The desire to keep their colours as brilliant as possible led the fauves to place less emphasis on outline than Gauguin and Van Gogh. In this respect it is highly instructive to compare Gauguin's *Vision after the Sermon (Pl. 154)* with Derain's *Hyde Park (Pl. 153)*. In the Gauguin, firm outlines coexist with elements of modelling; in the Derain the tints are unmodulated. Indeed in some instances there is no outline around the flat tint, which is defined only by the neighbouring colours. In their rejection of modelling, the fauves were rejecting *chiaroscuro*. They did not want to depict light; they wanted it to emanate from the colour itself, to form an integral part of its harmonies and brilliance.

As for the problem of space, even here they are not absolute innovators, but some of them, in particular Matisse, Derain, Friesz and Braque, do offer original solutions. They tend, in the main, to diminish depth so that they are constantly seen at least to weaken, if not to abolish, the convergence of lines. In addition, the colours they use for the background are usually as vivid as for the foreground; and in their landscapes they narrow the zone of the sky and occasionally do away with it altogether.

However, it is not enough to enumerate fauvism's contributions in order to demonstrate its historical importance; one must also stress the fact that it was a movement, for it was as such that it gave its contributions (and even those of its predecessors) a weight which two or three isolated artists could not have given them. It is for this reason that even painters who showed no great audacity are not without a certain value from the point of view of the history of art. By taking part in the movement, they enlarged its scope of action, and helped the new ideas to spread and to take root; and in this respect perhaps their cautiousness made them more immediately effective than the daring of their colleagues; it will be remembered that, at the outset, the leading fauves shocked and frightened more than they persuaded.

155 Derain Wood engraving for Apollinaire's ' L'ENCHANTEUR POURRISSANT ' 1909

The Dissolution of the Movement

It is natural that an artistic movement should last only a few years. The reasons which lead artists, at the outset of their careers, to band together for mutual support, and to present a united front to the hostility of the public, are reasons which disappear as soon as certain battles have been fought, certain obstacles overcome. In addition, with the passage of time, everyone becomes aware of what separates his personality from that of his comrades, and it is natural that he should henceforward feel impelled to follow his own bent independently of the others. For the impressionist group, the moment of dispersal came in 1883, that is to say after the movement had been going for ten years. As for fauvism, which displayed such youthful vitality and bouyancy in 1905, it ceased to exist, as we have seen, as early as 1908. Furthermore, while none of the artists who gathered together under the banner of impressionism ever radically changed direction, some of the principal representatives of fauvism not only parted from their comrades but turned their backs on their own past.

In 1908 the flames died down, in Vlaminck's and Derain's work as in Braque's and Friesz's. No more reds, or at least no more exultant reds; instead we have browns, ochres, greys, greens, muted blues. If during the fauve period these artists had sometimes given themselves over totally to the pleasures of the senses, now they became ascetic, austere; intoxication gave way to abstinence, rapture to discipline. They began to heed the teaching of Cézanne, whom Vlaminck called 'a sad friend of ours'. A retrospective exhibition at the Salon d'Automne of 1907, comprising fifty or so of Cézanne's works, focussed attention on his art once again. The publication at the same time of his letters to Emile Bernard gave prominence to his aesthetic opinions and gave rise to reflection on that sentence which was soon to become famous: 'Let me repeat what I have said here before: "Treat nature in terms of cylinder, sphere and cone, all drawn in perspective."'

However, one can only undergo an influence which one is ready to accept. How were the fauves impelled to follow Cézanne instead of Van Gogh and Gauguin? How did they explain their *volte-face*, or, if you prefer it, their conversion? Braque's reply was that 'it would be impossible to remain in a permanent state of paroxysm'. Vlaminck said: 'The play of pure colours, the exaggerated orchestration into which I had thrown myself heart and soul no longer satisfied me. I felt frustrated at being unable to strike yet harder, at having reached the maximum of intensity, restricted as I was by the blue or the red supplied by the paint shop.' Derain, for his part, told Georges Duthuit: 'What was wrong with our starting point

156
Dufy
L'ESTAQUE
1908

was that in a way we were afraid to imitate life; this led us to take too distant a view of reality, and to rush into ill-thought-out solutions. Where there is individuality there can be no imitation. So we have had to return to more moderate paths, to build up reserves at the outset in order to allow the picture a long and patient development. Nowadays I no longer believe in colour combinations. The mind alone should animate the work, even when there is almost nothing on the canvas: look at some of Rembrandt's portraits. The most lifeless and dull colour can be charged with limitless energy. The masters have an intangible power which goes beyond mere technique. Raphael, Rembrandt or Dürer: there is the divine gift.'

According to Braque, Vlaminck and Derain, then, fauvism was simply a blind alley: further progress was impossible unless they turned back on their tracks. But when they did turn back, did they really advance? In the case of Braque, who became one of the pioneers of cubism, there can be no possible doubt. With his love of 'the rule which corrects emotion', it would have been impossible for him to find a better means of fulfilment than the muted palette of his new speculative manner. Derain too began by choosing to paint in a static, geometrical style which was not unrelated to that of the cubists; but while the latter were analysing objects so closely that they caused them to fly apart, re-creating the visible world through a radical rejection of realistic conventions, Derain merely simplified or altered the external aspect of objects. He stretched the bodies and lengthened the faces, giving grave, stern, even grief-stricken expressions to his figures. This period, stretching from 1912 to 1914, was called his 'Gothic' period. If the canvases are less revolutionary than Braque's, they nonetheless have an indisputably modern air. Much the same is true of Vlaminck's and Friesz's work during their Cézannian period. Although they give us muted compositions which have been done with greater or lesser reflections and discipline, one can still detect traces of their former fire. But this period came to an end a few years later; and after

158
Derain
ROAD
TO BEAUVAIS
1911

1918 they went back to a traditionalist manner of painting, each artist doing no more than add a spice of his own.

Between the wars, people tried to give a universal significance to these repentances, especially Derain's, delighting in seeing in them a condemnation of the 'excesses'—in other words, the most interesting and characteristic properties—of modern painting. This condemnation was considered to be all the more final because it came from an artist who was universally recognized as one of the principal exponents of modernism. There is a genuine problem here, but it is more Derain's problem than that of modern art. Derain's letters to Vlaminck throw valuable light on this matter:

they show him as a man assailed by anxieties and doubts. One has the impression that he constantly needed to force himself, first of all to work, then to believe in the value of his work. He did, certainly experience moments of self-confidence, as when he announced in 1905 that he would be coming back from Collioure with 'some significant tips on colour'. But more often he would write like this: 'I am working... in a hopeless sort of way. I can never recognize it as mine and I don't know what I shall get out of it. Not much, if things go on as they are now.' And scarcely had he written: 'I am in the south. I'm happier here than I have ever been,' when we read in another letter: 'Work isn't going well. I can feel that I'm heading for another breakdown. ' In 1902, when he was in the army, he had written: 'It would seem from what has gone before that true othodoxy would teach us to belong to our own time; but this is a complicated business, and to be quite sure, I prefer to belong to all time.' Might it not be this desire to 'belong to all time' that explains Derain's evolution? Might he not have concluded that, as museum art has conquered eternity, by drawing nearer to it one may create works which will themselves be eternal? Everything suggests that this is so. And yet Derain's whole development is a refutation of this belief. Derain looked to the seventeenth-century Bolognese and Dutch schools, Poussin, Corot and the painters of ancient Rome; but by taking the old masters of realism as his models he weakened his own creative powers and the persuasive force of his painting. And if he has a place in the great tradition of European painting, it is much less for his traditionalist works than for his fauve pictures, because it is here that he is most personal and most inspired.

What is true of Derain also applies to Friesz and Vlaminck, although Vlaminck never ceased, even after 1918, to produce pictures which have a power to convince and to move (whenever his taste for drama and violence did not lead him into a facile and overstated lyricism). Those who deserted the fauvist cause were mistaken in believing that they had exhausted all the possibilities of pure colour; they had only exhausted the ones they had seen themselves. There were others, as Matisse and Dufy were to prove, Matisse throughout his career and Dufy from the moment he fully grasped his own originality.

160
Heckel
Two Men at a Table
1913

161
Schmidt-Rottluff
Seated Woman
1913

Influences and Parallel Trends

In the same year in which fauvism received its name in Paris, an analogous movement began to appear in Germany. This had its origin in an association founded in 1905 by four architecture students at the Technische Hochschule (technological university) in Dresden, Ernst-Ludwig Kirchner, Fritz Bleyl, Erich Heckel and Karl Schmidt-Rottluff. Kirchner and Bleyl had begun their studies at the school in 1901; they met in 1902. The others had met in Chemnitz in 1901, but Heckel did not come to Dresden to study until 1904 and Schmidt-Rottluff did not arrive until 1905. All, except perhaps Kirchner, were self-taught artists, with a passion for art and a sense of mission. The fauves bore a name which they had been given; but the young painters of Dresden themselves chose the name under which they appeared before the public: *Die Brücke* ('the bridge'). This was intended to express their desire for unity among themselves and their desire to see other artists joining them. The fauves were linked by friendship alone; *Die Brücke* was a group which believed in the value of close contacts and corporate work. The founders of *Die Brücke* met frequently in Kirchner's or Heckel's studio, as much to exchange ideas as to draw and paint figure studies untrammelled by the academic norms. The association included active and passive members, and for the benefit of the latter a year-book was published containing engravings and a report on the activities of the group. In 1906 they also published a manifesto formulated and engraved on wood by Kirchner; it consists of two sentences.

'Believing as we do in evolution, in a new generation of creators and enjoyers of art, we appeal to the young; being young, and being the bearers of the future, we desire to win from our comfortably established elders freedom to act and to live. Anyone who expresses his creative impulse directly and honestly is one of us.'

As Schmidt-Rottluff wrote in 1906, in the letter which induced Emil Nolde to join the group, the aim of *Die Brücke* was to attract all those who were in the state of revolt or ferment. The same year, 1906, saw the recruitment of Max Pechstein, the Swiss Cuno Amiet and the Finn Axel Gallen-Kalela. A year later Franz Nölken from Hamburg was persuaded to join. With the exception of Pechstein, these artists did not remain affiliated to *Die Brücke* for long: Nolde, who did not like being enrolled in a movement, left as early as 1907, followed in 1909 by Bleyl, who gave up his artistic activities at this time. On the other hand, 1910 marked a new (and final) admission to the group: that of Otto Müller. Amiet and Gallen-Kalela were not the only foreigners with whom the group sought contact; Pechstein had met Van Dongen in Paris in 1907, and in 1908 the latter was invited to take part in a *Die Brücke* show; he sent in a few works, but he was not accounted a member.

The first *Die Brücke* exhibition, including pictures by Bleyl, Heckel, Kirchner, Nolde, Pechstein and Schmidt-Rottluff, was put on in the showrooms of an electric lamp factory in Dresden in 1906. It attracted few visitors and little attention from the press. The following year the same artists, joined by Amiet, Gallen-Kalela and Nölken, put on a further collective exhibition in Dresden, but this time they were in one of the most prominent Dresden galleries, the Galerie Richter, and they attracted more attention. They were given the same reception as the fauves; they shocked and annoyed and were insulted. But, like the fauves, they would not allow themselves to be put off by their detractors; convinced that they were right and that their attackers were wrong, they continued their experiments and re-affirmed their positions. During the winter months they worked in Dresden, but during the summer they left the town to go and paint together in the country, most often in the region of the Moritzburg lakes in Saxony. They took their girl friends with them and painted them bathing or frolicking naked in the meadows and under the trees, thus compounding the revolt against academicism with a revolt against the prohibitions of current morality. In this respect they differ from the fauves, whose pre-occupations—except in the case of Vlaminck—were purely artistic.

In 1910 Heckel, Kirchner and Schmidt-Rottluff, together with Amiet, Müller and Pechstein, held a final exhibition at the Galerie

162
Munch
THE CRY
1893

Arnold in Dresden, still without managing to persuade the public
to come and see them. Material difficulties were an incitement to
settle elsewhere. Pechstein had already been settled in Berlin since
1908, as was Otto Müller; Heckel, Kirchner and Schmidt-Rottluff
decided to join them. They arrived towards the end of 1911.
Herwarth Walden defended them in his periodical *Der Sturm* ('the
tempest'), and slowly the number of their admirers grew. But
dissensions appeared within the group. In 1912 Pechstein was
excluded because, in disregard of a corporate decision, he had taken
part in an exhibition of the Berlin *Secession* on his own. A year later,
Kirchner wrote his *Chronik der Brücke,* which met with the approval
neither of Heckel nor of Müller and Schmidt-Rottluff. In consequence, there arose a disagreement which led to the group's dissolution: from now on everyone worked on his own, emphasizing what
was idiosyncratic in his own manner.

Does this mean that up to now the founders of the association had
had a common style? At the outset of their career they did, it is
true, present certain affinities of style; these are easily explained by

their preoccupations as well as by their 'ancestry'. Which of the artists who preceded them influenced their development? In some cases, the same men whose influence had been at work on the fauves: Van Gogh, Gauguin, Toulouse-Lautrec, the neo-impressionists, the masters of the Japanese print. Doubtless they knew some of these works only from reproductions in periodicals, but others they had seen at exhibitions. In 1902 the Galerie Arnold had shown some French impressionists and neo-impressionists, and in 1905 some Van Goghs. Kirchner, moreover, had visited a collective exhibition of neo-impressionist paintings in Munich in 1904. During the same year, in the Ethnographisches Museum in Dresden, he made the exciting discovery of sculpture from the Pellew Islands, and his colleagues were quick to share his enthusiasm. (At the same period in France, Matisse, Derain and Vlaminck were deeply moved and interested by Negro sculpture.) In addition, the *Die Brücke* painters studied the German masters of the sixteenth century, in particular Cranach, Grünewald and Dürer, and early woodcuts inspired them to do forceful and striking wood engravings. There is also a contemporary artist who must be regarded as one of their direct precursors: the Norwegian Edvard Munch, whose work had been known in Germany since 1892. The morbid and anguished character of his art at the turn of the century does indeed find an echo in more than one of the Dresden painters' canvases.

It would be impossible to say at what moment they came across fauve works, but their evolution, and especially Kirchner's, proves that Matisse's art was not unknown to them in 1908. Perhaps they knew Matisse only in reproduction; but in 1907 they had had access to a livelier source of information when Pechstein returned from his stay in Paris. This information was not merely verbal; Matisse's experiments find an echo in Pechstein's own works.

It is difficult to gain an accurate idea of Kirchner's early career as an artist. He seems to have antedated some of his paintings, so that one can place little faith in the information which he himself supplies. However, as he signed the date 1906 on certain works, one is entitled to assume that they were not completed before that year. While his vision remains impressionist, that is to say, while Kirchner shows great sensivity not only to light and atmosphere but also to the more amiable side of the external world, the long broad

163
Kirchner
YOUNG GIRL
WITH BLUE DIVAN
1907–8

brushstrokes jostle against each other in places and the colour tends to have a life of its own. This independence is real enough in the *Young Girl with Ruff* (H.H. Thyssen–Bornemisza collection) where the purples, greens and blues of the face, the reds and purples of the hair are obviously invented colours, where the colour composition has lost its idyllic quality and the emphatic strokes betray the underlying impatience.

Can it really be that it was also in 1906 that Kirchner painted the *Nude with Japanese Parasol* (Stuttgarter Kunstkabinett)? If the answer is yes, then it must be said that he has skipped several stages, for here the juxtaposition of numerous small rectangles of colour gives way to several zones of colours which are almost flat tints, hence a painting which is less 'restless' than before, but which is no less intense. The draughtsmanship has changed too, becoming clearer and more calligraphic; the contour has taken on the appearance of an arabesque, and the volumes tend to flatten out. Perhaps we should see in this change the influence of the Japanese print or of Toulouse-Lautrec, but there is also the fact that, like his colleagues, Kirchner was doing wood-engravings, and the flattened forms which his technique led him to create found their way into his paintings. Unmodulated colours can be seen in works like the *Artist and his Model (Pl. 181)* and *Young Girl with Blue Divan (Pl. 163)* —the dates are given as 1907-8—where the forms really look as if they have been defined with a knife. The colour composition has, for its part, become more violent. It has acquired a categorical quality and the harmonies are not without harshness.

Besides the girls, clothed or unclothed, whom he presents in interiors *(Two Nudes, Pl. 185)*, Kirchner painted nudes against a landscape, female nudes for the most part, but sometimes with a male nude by their side. In neither case does he reduce the bodies to arabesques as does Matisse. While simplifying the anatomy, covering the forms in orange, green, blue or red tones, in other words removing them from the sphere of naturalistic representation,

164
Kirchner
NUDE IN STUDIO
1910-11

he does not make purely decorative elements of them. He always presents them in such a way as to carry a hint of eroticism, and the same is true to a certain extent even when the subject is a cabaret or circus scene, with men and women dancing stiffly round. He delights in such subjects because they allow him to paint movements, and also because of the importance he attached to all forms of escape from bourgeois life and all forms of revolt against it.

Whilst the rural landscapes bring us into contact with human beings living without constraint, in a natural environment from which they draw new strength, his urban landscapes confront us with a very different atmosphere. Sometimes the city appears as an artificial environment where concrete and metal have more reality than the trees, and where man is merely a passer-by moving in a cold vacuum (*The Railway Bridge at Löbtau*, 1907—private collection). At other times we can see nothing but a motley crowd walking along a pink highway (*Dresden street*, 1907, *Pl. 166*).

Cramped together by the picture frame, which it constantly seems to be trying to spill over, this crowd appears ill at ease, notwithstanding the fashionable dresses which the women are showing off. It is true that one cannot read in their faces the anguish and torture of the city dwellers in Munch's pictures, but a disquiet inhabits even these gaudy masks of clashing reds and greens.

When Kirchner left Dresden for Berlin, he made almost no changes in his subjects, but he did concentrate more on form. He elongates the bodies, making them more geometric and defining them with an outline, and often uses hatchings to produce the modelling. This style, denoting a (superficial) influence of cubism, and which occasionally takes on a jerky appearance, is particularly suited to depicting further street scenes, more original and more striking than those from Dresden. Women wearing exaggerated fashions and elegantly dressed men, walking affectedly and trying to show off, make up a strange fauna which the artist evokes with perhaps more irritation than amusement. Kirchner's tall and angular figures are at this period similar to those which Derain at about the same time

166 Kirchner DRESDEN STREET 1907

167
Kirchner
THE STREET
1913

was introducing into the pictures of his 'Gothic' period. The colour in Kirchner's Berlin canvases has, as a rule, less brilliance than that of the Dresden pictures, but this is only a temporary muting of the artist's palette. About 1918, he went back to brighter colour harmonies, and basically he retained his liking for them for the rest of his life. The landscapes and interiors which he subsequently painted in Switzerland are full of pinks, purples, blues, greens which are notable for their insistent purity.

Heckel for his part began to work in a manner denoting the influence of the neo-impressionists and Van Gogh. In his works of

1907 the juxtaposed brushstrokes occasionally mingle and overlap, and the application of the paint seems even more violent and impetuous than Kirchner's. Two years later, in the *Nude on a Sofa* *(Pl. 168)*, the line is no longer fragmented; swarms of dots have been succeeded by fields of colour which look purer than before because they are less at variance with each other. There is nothing particularly sensual about the nude woman except that she is hiding her face in her hands, and this gesture, which seems to stem from the feigned modesty of love play, is such that we see more than mere pictorial reality in the nude. Amongst the fauves, Van Dongen alone gives a similar significance to the unclothed form, whereas in the *Die Brücke* painters (discreet) erotic references are frequent.

From 1908 to 1910 Heckel painted landscapes, especially at Dangast in Oldenburg, where he joined Schmidt-Rottluff. Vibrant colours, applied with verve, forms hastily suggested with a broad brush, and an acrid atmosphere in spite of the blue sky, these charac-

168 Heckel NUDE ON A SOFA 1909

169
Heckel
MILL
AT DANGAST
1909

170
Heckel
FASANEN-
SCHLÖSSCHEN
1910

terize the *Mill at Dangast,* 1909 *(Pl. 169).* However, Heckel is lighter and less vehement than Schmidt-Rottluff. Indeed, a feeling of calm emanates from some of his works of this period, particularly the *Fasanenschlösschen (Hunting Lodge),* 1910 *(Pl. 170)* where the obvious brushstrokes are replaced by a smooth, even surface. For the rest, the artist is still chiefly concerned with the construction of the picture, and although his technique may seem hasty, his painting does not lack reflection, a fact which one fully realizes on looking at the painting *At the Pond in the Wood* (Buchheim collection, Feldafing), also done in 1910. Here the arrangement is most deliberate; the nudes are grouped with a view to their decorative effect,

171
Heckel
BROTHER AND SISTER
1911

172 Heckel Two Men by a Table 1912

their forms complementing the drawing of the pond and the contours of the foliage. But the colouring is far from being bucolic in
character: as though a stormy sky is darkening the pond, the light
reveals an indefinable sense of disquiet. It was in the same year,
1910, that Heckel did the portrait of *Pechstein Asleep* (Buchheim
collection, Feldafing), with its reds, blues, saturated greens, each
colour placed so as to contrast with its neighbour. Since in addition
the form is vigorously emphasized, the whole has a somewhat rough
appearance once more.

In *Brother and Sister (Pl. 171)*, which Heckel painted in 1911,
probably after moving to Berlin, the draughtsmanship is more
geometric than it had been previously: the contours are stressed
and tend to break whilst describing sharp angles. Here again, as
in Kirchner's work, cubism or the cubistic painting of Feininger,
Marc and Macke, with whom Heckel now came in contact, has
something to do with his new trend. The colour is muted, one

might even call it cold and saddened. Sadness and an anxious medita-
tion are equally discernible in the eyes, indeed in the whole expression of the faces: an anxiety which becomes anguish in the *Two
Men by a Table* of 1912 *(Pl. 172)*. One sees why the artist gave the
additional title *To Dostoyevsky* to this canvas: when looking at it,
it is hard not to be reminded of the sufferings and oppressions of
Dostoyevsky's characters. There is even something disquieting
about the *Harbour at Stralsund* of 1912 *(Pl. 173)*, in spite of the fact
that there is no lack of either pinks or reds. Other works of the
same period and the following years are less vivid in colouring; time
only served to increase the distance between Heckel's painting and
that of the fauves.

Of all the artists of *Die Brücke*, Schmidt-Rottluff is the one who
offers the most strength and ruggedness, as he demonstrated in 1906
in a *Self-Portrait (Pl. 174)*, where it is difficult to discern the face

173 Heckel HARBOUR AT STRALSUND 1912

174
Schmidt-Rottluff
SELF-PORTRAIT
1906

in the general effect of thick, writhing, closely-packed brushstrokes.
A *Self-Portrait with Monocle* of 1910 *(Pl. 175)* is even more significant.
The summarily modulated flat tint replaces the technique inherited
from Van Gogh. The simplification of the form, the freedom of
the colour harmonies denote a temperament not averse to brutality.
The colour composition is no less free, the draughtsmanship is no
less summary in *Rest in the Studio (Pl. 184)* and the *Farm at Dangast*
(Galerie des 20. Jahrhunderts, Berlin), which also date from 1910.
But it was during the summer of the following year, when Schmidt-
Rottluff was working in Norway, that his colour reached its peak
of intensity. Whether he took as his subject houses near a fjord
(Lofthus, Pl. 176), or a valley surrounded by mountains *(Strydedal,*
Buchheim collection, Feldafing), objects are reduced to blocks
differentiated by violent colours: an elemental sturdiness and a
harsh gravity characterize these works. A year later, in Berlin, the

influence of Negro art, and doubtless that of cubism, manifest themselves in the artist's work. Indeed, he had always made a cult of primitivism, but now his forms become even more geometrical. Objects are defined by stiff outlines; the colouring is occasionally less vivid. Thus in 1913 Schmidt–Rottluff painted *Three Red Nudes* (Galerie des 20. Jahrhunderts, Berlin), their massive forms are enclosed by a few rudimentary curves. There is no concern for physical beauty; these women remain close to the earth whose fertility is evoked by their heavy breasts, their wide hips and their generous bulk. Schmidt–Rottluff kept this manner, with its deliberate simplifications, during and after the war years, although making less aggressive alterations as time went by.

Pechstein played, in relation to the founders of *Die Brücke,* a similar role to that of Manguin in relation to a fauve such as Matisse. Although he was influenced by the latter, Pechstein diverged less from the realist tradition than his colleagues, and although he used

176
Schmidt–Rottluff
LOFTHUS
1911

177
Schmidt–Rottluff
PINE TREES
IN FRONT OF
WHITE HOUSE
1911

181

178 Nolde THE LAST SUPPER 1910

a vivid palette, his temperament was less wild and passionate than theirs. The result was that he outraged the public less than his colleagues did and was the first to win public acceptance.

Although one cannot deny that Otto Müller has more originality than Pechstein, he is nevertheless far from being a Kirchner or a Schmidt–Rottluff. Müller's art lacks violence; in particular, his use of colour lacks brilliance, as he uses a technique which excludes vivid sonorities *a priori,* tempera on a hessian canvas. Even his light colours have a muted dullness which alienates him from the spirit of fauvism—while his taste for geometrical form reveals cubist influence.

The violence unknown in Otto Müller's work is the primary characteristic of Emil Nolde's. The latter was almost forty when he joined *Die Brücke* but, although he had been working for a decade, he had not yet evolved his own personal manner. A vision and a technique obviously reminiscent of impressionism are found even as late as the canvases he painted in 1907. *Wildly Dancing Children* of

1909 (Kunsthalle, Kiel) also retains the luminosity of the impressionists, but the very summary notation of the bodies, the violent handling, the gashes of colour, scarcely suggesting a consistent form, all this indicates that the painter is at a turning point of his development. In fact the following year he did *The Last Supper (Pl. 178)*, in which impressionism is not merely rejected but totally forgotten. What we have here is simply a projection on to the canvas of the artist's sensitivity and imagination. No doubt the basic inspiration for these clumsy figures came from the peasants Nolde saw in his native Schleswig, but the ecstasy on their faces is the product of the artist's own ardent, primitive, rustic religious faith, which he expresses in an idiom which could hardly be more crude: a hurriedly sketched form, garish colours, a paint surface which denies the slightest pleasure to an eye taken with sensual charms. In his quest

179 Nolde Dance around the Golden Calf 1910

180 Nolde Tropical Sun 1914

for expressive power, Nolde makes no attempt to avoid clashing colours, caricature, or even frank ugliness.

In 1910 he took up the theme of open-air dancing once again, and this now became the *Dance around the Golden Calf (Pl. 179)*. From now on he ceased to concern himself with effects of light and there is little gradation in the body colours (yellows, purples, oranges) which in consequence lose some of their former flickering quality, while the forms are less fragmentary. The arrangement of the colours, as well as the increased clarity of the gestures, add to the emotive power of movements which it would be an understatement to call violent; they are frenetic. A third variation on this theme is provided in 1912 in the *Candle Dancers* (Nolde-Stiftung, Seebüll). Four figures were dancing up and down in each of the first two versions; in this last, only two are to be seen (which has made it possible to increase their size considerably): two girls dressed in full, billowing skirts, with breasts as well as arms and legs bared, their purplish flesh contrasting with a red and orange background. The earth, too, is red, thus accentuating the unreal quality of the scene.

The colours are so intense that they have an orgiastic, a delirious quality. This is also true of the forms; the bodies are mere rags shaken by uncontrollable convulsions.

Other canvases offer less violence, but scarcely more harmony. Even with the *Holiday Guests* (Galerie Hoffmann, Hamburg), which Nolde painted in 1911, the harmonies have a harsh and discordant quality which it is impossible to define. These dissonances are *a fortiori* intensified in those works which take as their subject café scenes observed in Berlin; here, seated at tables with glasses of wine which produce only a disgusting drunkenness, are people whose souls are a prey to emptiness or furtive savagery (*Slovenes*, 1911 *Pl. 186*); *Drinking Wine*, 1911, Nolde Stiftung, Seebüll). Nor are the landscapes more peaceful: the sea, for instance, becomes heavy, lashing waves advancing towards us beneath a green and orange sky.

In 1913, the German Colonial Office invited Nolde to make a trip to New Guinea, a project which he must have found all the more interesting in that for several years he had felt attracted by everything primitive. Thus it was that his *Tropical Sun* of 1914

182
Nolde
PAPUAN
FAMILY
1915

183
Nolde
FIGURE AND MASK
1911

(Pl. 180) or his *Papuan Family* of 1915 *(Pl. 182)* necessitated no change of manner on his part. Indeed, his style evolved very little further. All his life he was to be an exponent of vehemence, strident colour composition, coarse and apparently perfunctory technique. Although he had spent much of his life in towns, he remained a savage peasant, for whom strength of feelings took priority over a rich and refined sensitivity. By comparison with him, Vlaminck appears singularly tame, and his idiom acquires an almost studied refinement. As to his kinship with other fauves, in spite of the fact that Nolde's palette was similar to theirs, a gulf separated him from them, since he was completely unaware of the importance they

184
Schmidt-Rottluff
REST IN THE STUDIO
1910

185 Kirchner Two Nudes 1905

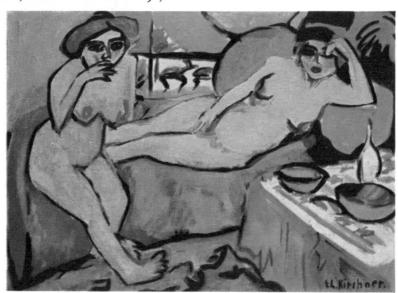

186
Nolde
SLOVENES
1911

187
Modersohn–Becker
NUDE GIRL
WITH FLOWERS
1907

attached to pictorial qualities. The only thing that mattered for him was to interpret his visions in a striking manner without concerning himself with the eloquence which is peculiar to a 'work of art'.

Other early twentieth-century German artists used a colour composition which is akin to that of the fauves. Paula Modersohn–Becker, before her early death in 1907, spent some time in Paris on different occasions; her most attractive works attest to her admiration for Gauguin *(Pl. 187)*. However, it was among those painters who were working in Munich that fauve affinities are the most clearly discernible, being particularly manifest in the work of the Russians Jawlensky and Kandinsky. Having arrived in the Bavarian capital in 1896, they met at Anton Azbé's art school where they had gone to continue studies begun in Russia. The very year of their arrival in Germany saw the appearance of the initial number of the review *Die Jugend* ('Youth'), which was to give its name to the *Jugendstil,* the German equivalent of the French *Style moderne* and the English Art Nouveau. In 1901 Kandinsky founded the *Phalanx* group over which he presided until 1904. He also taught in the school opened by the group in 1902. Their obvious aim was to bring to Munich a type of art different from the more or less traditional naturalism which had held sway until then, and which the *Jugendstil* also set out to challenge. Since the French impressionists were scarcely known to the Munich public, the moving spirits behind the *Phalanx* conceived the idea of putting on a Pissarro exhibition, but in view of the indifference which greeted their other activities, they were obliged to give up the idea. However, just before the dissolution of the group in 1904, they did put on the collective exhibition of neo-impressionists which Kirchner went to see. The same year, they had the satisfaction of seeing that elsewhere too people were becoming more receptive to new ideas: works by Cézanne, Gauguin and Van Gogh were accepted by the *Künstlerverein* (Society of artists). Jawlensky and Kandinsky were not content merely to admire French painting; they wanted to gain recognition for their own work in Paris; and so they sent pictures up to the Salon d'Automne, Kandinsky being accepted from 1904 onwards and Jawlensky in 1905. In addition, they both spent some time in France: Kandinsky lived in Sèvres from June 1906 to June 1907, although no one could really say that he was in direct contact

188
Jawlensky
WOMAN WITH FAN
1909

with the *avant-garde* of the time. Jawlensky, however, who visited Paris in 1903 and 1905, at the very moment that the fauve scandal erupted, made use of the opportunity to make Matisse's acquaintance.

He had already shown his liking for colour, but more and more his aim became to extol its purity. Like almost all the painters discussed in this book, he began by composing his pictures with the countless small strokes, for which he took his example from the impressionists. From there he went on to definite flat tints. Thus, in the *Mediterranean near Marseilles* of 1907 (Folkwang Museum, Essen), we have a teeming mass of dots applied with a broad brush, but also a tendency for colours to be arranged in groups so that they make up distinct and separate zones. The palette is less luminous

and light than that of the impressionists, but it is also more inventive,
being characterized by a warm quality which comes, not from the
world around the artist but from his own nature. The *Still-Life
with Yellow and White Pitchers* of 1908 (private collection, Locarno)
exemplifies quite a different manner. Here, each tint is isolated in a
field defined by an outline; and the reds, purples, whites and yellows
are all the more vivid because they rise from a blackish-blue background. The velvety splendour of this deep colour harmonizes
admirably with the light, high tones, giving them a radiance and at
the same time preserving them from any aggressive stridency. In the
Girl with Peonies of 1909 *(Pl. 190)* varying shades of pink and red,
which are generously spread out, are arranged to harmonize with
blues, greens, yellows; and here again the colour composition appeals
by its combination of richness, audacity and refinement. This is
also true of *The Red Shawl* dating from the same year, a work of

vigour, brilliance and freshness.   There was probably no other artist in Germany at this time whose colour *(Pl. 189)* was so original and at the same time so vibrant and harmonious.

The contour is little emphasized in *The Red Shawl,* but this is exceptional.   In 1910 Jawlensky began to place more and more emphasis on outline.   Moreover, with him the line is also a colour, often a light, intense, unmodelled blue.   At the same time that he was broadening his line, he stiffened it and made it resolutely geometric, so that his form became simplified, sculptural, and his faces took on a hieratic expression.   This desire for simplification often leads to a rather schematic effect.   All the evidence suggests that, in Jawlensky's case as with the founder members of *Die Brücke,*

190
Jawlensky
GIRL WITH PEONIES
1909

this tendency was inspired by cubism. It is also possible that Jawlensky felt the influence of popular art: the draughtsmanship, the somewhat naive purity of the colour composition, and the prominent staring eyes of the figures, are in fact reminiscent of the painting on glass which used to be practised in Bavaria and the Tyrol.

Some of the landscapes of 1910–14 are no less stylized than the figures. In one of them, the *Murnau Landscape* of 1912 (private collection, Hofheim/Taunus), the mountains are reduced by broad contours to a few circumscribed planes. Colour alone differentiates them, a pure sumptuous colour which gives the picture the vibrancy of stained glass.

The tendency towards geometrical shapes becomes more apparent in the heads Jawlensky painted in Switzerland during the First World War and later in Wiesbaden; it disappeared only during the artist's last years, when his hand, crippled with arthritis, had lost

191
Jawlensky
STILL-LIFE
WITH VASE
AND PITCHER
1909

its old dexterity. His colour did not lose all its brilliance after 1914, but its ardour became less apparent; although it still burns even in his most muted tints.

In 1905, at the beginning of his fauve period, Jawlensky was forty-one. Wassily Kandinsky was even older when, in Murnau, in Bavaria, in 1908, colour began to play a vital part in his work. In about 1907 the influence of *Jugendstil* had led him to abandon academic painting, and since then he had been in a state of tentative experiment. The canvases he painted during his stay in Sèvres (1906–7), especially those done in the park of Saint Cloud, are not very far from impressionism, except that the brushwork is broader and heavier, and also coarser than Monet's or Pissarro's. All this was changed at Murnau. The colour breaks free and becomes

autonomous; its own lyricism takes precedence over the details of the objects confronting the painter. In some pictures, a spirit of feverish excitment is present; the reds and yellows seem to be boiling. Here Kandinsky is still more fiery and impatient than Jawlensky, so that objects lose not only their colour but also their normal form and identity. Even more than in the Murnau landscapes, this is true in the canvases Kandinsky painted in 1909 from memories of a journey to Tunisia made five years earlier. Various of these works are called *Improvization (Pl. 194)* or *Composition*, and if here and there one can pick out figures, a wall, mountains, there are parts which it would be impossible to identify as objects. The eye takes in only brilliant, sundrenched colours, with here and there a touch of fairground jazziness which recalls the Russian popular art which had influenced Kandinsky's earlier pictures.

The low importance attached to the object in these paintings foreshadows the moment in 1910 when Kandinsky was to paint his first abstract painting. He now drew apart from the fauves who, whilst metamorphosing the visible world, never rejected it. But he retained his liking for pure colour, and highpitched harmonies were the distinguishing feature of his work before 1914.

In 1909 Kandinsky, together with Jawlensky, Adolf Erbslöh and Alexander Kanoldt, founded the *Neue Künstlervereinigung* ('new association of artists') of Munich, which opened its first exhibition in December 1909 at the Galerie Thannhäuser. The two Russians were not alone amongst these painters in adopting fauve mannerisms: in Erbslöh's *Nude with Garter* 1909 *(Pl. 195)* points of similarity with Matisse are immediately obvious. But the disapproval with which various members of the *Neue Künstlervereinigung* met Kandinsky's renunciation of representational art in 1911 led to his decision to found, together with Franz Marc, a new group which they called *Der Blaue Reiter* ('the blue horseman'). In company with Henri Rousseau, Delaunay, Macke, Campendonk and several

194 Kandinsky Improvization 14 1910

others, the two friends exhibited for the first time under the new name in December 1911, still at the Galerie Thannhäuser. Three months later they put on a collective exhibition of drawings and prints at the Galerie Goltz in which Paul Klee took part. Generally speaking, the members of the group were, in their aims and methods, as far from the fauves as from the *Die Brücke* expressionists. It is true that in Tegernsee in 1909-10 Macke painted figures, still-lifes and landscapes which are reminiscent of Matisse both in their colour composition and its decorative arrangement. Probably Marc too was acquainted with the French master; an exhibition of Matisse's work had been held in Munich in 1910, and Macke must have spoken of his enthusiasm to his friend. However, Marc strove to give a symbolic value to his colour harmonies, to express the tenderness with which he viewed animals, so that in about 1910-11 his position was nearer to the tradition of Van Gogh and Gauguin. In 1912 Marc and Macke visited Delaunay in Paris, and although like him they retained pure colours, their forms became progressively more geometrized and, in the construction of their pictures, they adopted a manner nearer to cubism than fauvism.

As well as the German painters whom Matisse influenced only remotely, there were those, such as Hans Purrmann, Oskar and Greta Moll, and Rudolf Levy, who came under his direct guidance in Paris. These were the students who attended the academy he opened in 1907 and directed until 1911. There were, amongst others, Americans (P.H. Bruce, Max Weber), Hungarians (Joseph Brummer, Bela Czobel), Swedes (Leander Engström, Isaac Grünewald and his wife Sigrid Hjertén, Nils von Dardel, Arthur Percy, Einar Jolin), Norwegians (Jean Heiberg, Per Krogh, Alex Revold, Henrik Sörensen), an Englishman (Matthew Smith), Austrians, Poles and Russians. More than a hundred of them came to listen to Matisse's teaching during the five years his school was open and, on their return to their own countries, they took with them the master's ideas. This did not mean that they accepted them unquestioningly; in their subsequent development, many rejected them to a greater or lesser extent. Purrmann was among those who did not forget what they had learnt in Paris. In his interiors, his still-lifes and his flower pieces, he showed a sense of decorative composition which immediately indicates the influence which sharpened it, although his draughtsmanship and colour harmonies reveal a different sensitivity from that of the French painter whom he took as his model.

Matthew Smith's contacts with Matisse were brief, since he did not enter the academy until 1911, when it was about to be closed, but he was nonetheless influenced by the fauve painter's art. It is true that before coming to Paris, Smith had admired Gauguin (his first stop on his arrival in France had been at Pont-Aven) and later he was to worship Rubens and Delacroix as well as Renoir and Cézanne. The studies of nudes and flowers he painted in London in 1916 are distinguished by the brilliance of the colour, with its abundance of definite reds (contrasting, in the nudes, with decidedly green shadows), the clarity of draughtsmanship, and the insistence

195
Erbslöh
NUDE
WITH GARTER
1909

of the contours *(Nude, Fitzroy Street, no. 1, Pl. 196)*. Smith's draughtsmanship is reminiscent of another master for whom he had evinced an appreciative interest, Ingres, as much as of Matisse. The colour is no less transposed, the form scarcely less affirmed in the Cornwall landscapes dating from 1920. On the other hand, in the nude studies which he painted a few years later in Paris, the tension of the line is relaxed, the bodies have lost their sculptural quality, the brushwork broadens out and spreads the colour with a sort of abandon. The nudes are lying full length on bed covers in front of coloured hangings, their soft, opulent flesh marrying its orange and pink tones with the reds of the materials; few cold tones inter-vene to challenge their exuberance of colour *(Couleur de Rose,* 1924, British Council collection). Women lying on a bed, with heavy breasts bared, reappear in some of his works of 1930–31, but these

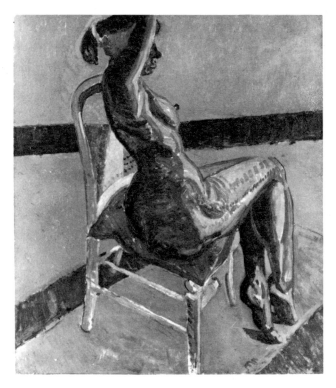

196
Matthew Smith
NUDE,
FITZROY STREET, no 1
1916

197
Matthew
Smith
WOMAN
WITH ROSE
1930

198
Wouters
RED CURTAINS
1913

latter present more contrasts and—in fine—more richness *(Woman with Rose, Pl. 197)*. Shortly afterwards, the artist settled in Provence where he used a more limited palette in his landscapes whilst his handling seems even more violent and impetuous. Smith also liked to paint still-lifes; a taste for brilliantly-coloured tablecloths remained with him throughout his life.

The Belgian Rik Wouters never met Matisse and had little appreciation for his pictures. But his study of Ensor, Cézanne, Van Gogh and Renoir led him, especially after 1912, to paint canvases akin to those of the fauves. Whether he was painting pears scattered on a table *(Still-life with Fruit, 1912, Musées Royaux des Beaux-Arts, Brussels)* or his wife at home *(Portrait of Mme Rik Wouters, 1912, Musée National d'Art Moderne, Paris; Red Curtains, 1913, Pl. 198)*, or a self-portrait in which he depicts himself with a black bandage over his right eye *(Self-Portrait, 1915, Dr L. Van Bogaert collection, Antwerp)*, he brings pure colours into play and gives an ample lyricism to his reds. However, although Wouter's colours are warm, they are also somewhat softened; although he communicates feelings of joy, one can also discern elements of nostalgia in his work, especially when he portrays his wife. Although he likes to clothe her in red jackets and dresses, she has a delicate and sickly quality which contrasts oddly with the gaiety of the colouring. For the rest, the painter is too distinguished a colourist to be satisfied with a crude palette. In his work refinement and passion combine with the utmost ease and spontaneity. Wouters, who died in 1916, enjoyed only four years in which to realize the major part of his work—and during the war his life was further uprooted by fighting, internment in Holland and illness. And yet he has won recognition as a rich and delightful colourist and as one of the most attractive of twentieth-century Belgian artists.

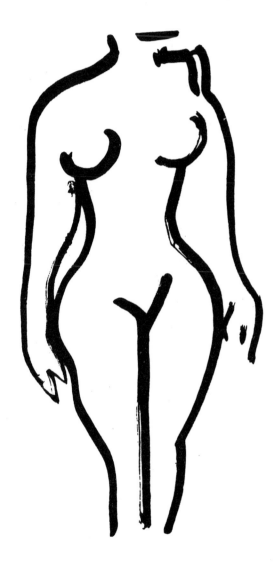

The Survival of Fauvism

We have looked at Matisse's development as far as 1907. There is
nothing to indicate that the crisis which almost all the fauves under-
went that year had any effect on him. In the face of an ever-growing
number of desertions, he did not swerve from his course. Not only
did he publish in 1908 his 'Notes d'un Peintre', in which, as we
have already seen, he expounded his ideas with freshness and intelligence, he also painted a work in which it seems as though he was

trying to show that fauvism had in no way lost its dynamism. He took as his subject, *The Dessert,* which he had already treated thirteen years before (Edward G. Robinson collection, Hollywood), transposing it radically in his new manner. In 1897, he had made great use of *chiaroscuro* and tonal values to express himself: the light, which comes in through the window in the background, falls on a table laden with cutlery, flasks and fruit dishes; the light, now definite, now reflected off an object, grows dimmer and fades while leaving the form and substance of objects unaltered. The illusion of depth, on the other hand, emerges quite unequivocally; produced in the first place by the situation of the table which, cut in half in the foreground, juts out obliquely into the room, leaving a gap between itself and the partition in the background. Little remains of all that in *The Dessert, Red Harmony* (also called *The Red Room*) of 1908 *(Pl. 201)*. Here the light does not give the impression of progression, notwithstanding the presence of a window through which a landscape bathed in light can be seen. Nor are there any shadows. Simply colours, and they give the work its luminosity. The dominant colour is red, covering with an equal intensity the cloth on the table and the wall in the background. Its purity remains unaltered, except for a blue floral pattern which appears on the wall as well as on the tablecloth. It would hardly be possible to distinguish a third dimension were it not for several elements which make it perceptible: two identical chairs, of which one is on a smaller scale than the other; a woman behind the table, separating the two plain surfaces with a red. The flat tint which predominates in the room is echoed in the landscape, where the third dimension is indicated in a similar manner. A pink house intervenes, between the blue of the sky and the green of a meadow planted with whitish-leaved trees, and it is the smallness of the house in relation to the trees that makes us aware of a distance. Thus in this work Matisse rejects both linear and spatial perspective, totally abolishing the naturalistic manner in favour of the 'decorative manner' of which he speaks in his *Notes*.

He used the same technique when in 1909 he painted *The Dance (Pl. 203)*. Only four tones are used in this work: a blue, a green, two brick reds (a pale one for the naked bodies of the dancers and a dark one for the hair and the contours). Doubtless the function of the blue is to suggest the sky, and the green, the hill where the round dance is being performed, but above all each tone has its own intrinsic value. It has an existential rather than a representational quality. Since the forms are simply defined by the line which encloses the bodies and emphasizes their lively movement, the flat tints have an absolute purity. Never before had Matisse achieved such a degree of economy and vibrancy, never had he displayed such candour in the use of colour, or drawn so much brilliance from such a limited palette.

Furthermore, *The Dance* is no ordinary picture. It measures no less than 2.60 × 3.90 m. and Matisse planned it to be hung on a staircase in the Moscow mansion of Sergei Shchukin, the Russian collector who was one of his chief patrons. *The Dessert, Red Harmony* was also intended as a 'decorative panel' for the same patron's dining-room. This function at least partly explains the simplified manner of these works by comparison with smaller and more intimate pictures of the same period. Thus, the *Algerian Girl* of 1909 (Musée National

201 Matisse THE DESSERT, RED HARMONY 1908

d'Art Moderne, Paris) displays modelled surfaces next to flat tints, and the form is not consistently outlined. The colour, however, is still vivid and the draughtsmanship vigorous. In the *Girl with Black Cat* of 1910 (private collection, France), the stiff frontal position of the model gives an air of severity, and the colouring is more restrained, without being any less distinguished or impressive. Matisse refused to seek one single solution for the problems he set himself; but he nevertheless maintained his chosen course.

He was encouraged in this by two exhibitions of Muslim art, one in Munich in 1910 and the other in Paris in 1912. The Persian miniatures which he admired there confirmed him in his belief that, where colour retains its force and draughtsmanship its clarity, where one can perceive (although not measure) distance, painting can combine exquisite sensitivity and refined spirituality. A visit to Moscow in 1911 revealed to him the world of icons, and helped to strengthen his convictions. Other travels—in Spain (1911) and Morocco (1911-12 and 1912-13)—gave him ideas for new themes and new harmonies (*Zorah in Yellow*, private collection, Chicago).

During these same years Matisse also painted glowing still-lifes and interiors. As in *The Dessert, Red Harmony* his aim was to reconcile unmodelled tints with a notation of space which, although not insistent, was nonetheless highly expressive. In the *Red Studio*, done in 1911 (Museum of Modern Art, New York) the same red tone almost completely covers the surface of the picture, covering indiscriminately the floor and the walls, as well as a table and chair, a chest of drawers, a clock. The few other colours which interrupt the monochrome are, generally speaking, less solid and lighter than the dominant colour, being for the most part confined within the

203 Matisse THE DANCE 1910

paintings hanging on the wall or placed on the floor. Moreover, if the floor and the wall are distinguishable, it is above all by virtue of the proportional relationships of the objects; it is also because of several oblique lines, very unobtrusively drawn, which direct the gaze into the centre of the picture. But the eye can never be certain that it can penetrate into the picture: the effect of the red colouring is to make spatial depth seem to disappear at the very moment that it reveals itself to us, so that we are left with the impression of seeing space continually expanding and contracting, which gives a brilliant and striking, and at the same time mysterious and subtle, life to the picture.

It was doubtless the atmosphere generated by cubism that led Matisse in about 1913 to tone down his palette and to turn towards a more disciplined art; but although he made form geometrical, he never went so far as to fragment it, nor did he ever restrict his palette to greys and ochres. This tendency in Matisse was most marked in 1916–17, when he painted *The Piano Lesson (Pl. 204)*, one of his most daring, free and 'abstract' works.

Between 1918 and 1930 a certain slackening of effort is noticeable in his work. On going to live in Nice, Matisse yielded to the charms of light. One might almost say that he was seeking some form of compromise with the principles of realism. In any case, he became more amenable and clashed less with convention. His finest paintings of this period are the *Odalisques:* with their echoes of the time he spent in Morocco, these are powerful evocations of Oriental languor, sensuality and refinement, retaining a richness and freshness of colour as well as a rare distinction in their colour harmonies *(Odalisque with Tambourine, Pl. 200)*.

The Dance, done in 1931–3 for the Barnes Foundation in Merion, Pennsylvania (a first version is in the Petit Palais in Paris), presents us with a bolder and more austere art. Basically this monumental composition marks the beginning of a revival of authentic fauvism. Matisse was completely aware of this; in 1936, he declared to Teriade: 'When the means have been refined to such an extent that their expressive power is diminished, one must get back to the basic principles which formed human language; then they will come to life and give us life. Pictures made up of refinements, subtle gradations, melting transitions call for beautiful blues, beautiful reds and

beautiful yellows, substances which move the sensual basis of man's nature. That's the starting point of fauvism: the courage to find what is pure in the means... In my most recent pictures I have grafted what I have gained during the last twenty years on to what is fundamental in my art—and in myself.'

Indeed, if the new fauvism can be distinguished from the old, it is above all by its maturity. The painter now transposes nature, not only more authoritatively than before but also with greater facility. Lengthy studies and a great many drawings have enabled him to master objects so completely that henceforward he can define them with a single line without the risk of giving them a diagrammatic appearance. His colours are no less brilliant than during the fauve period, but they are more refined, more distinctive and more luminous. They are also richer, although the colour range is sometimes restricted. Matisse is tireless in varying his colour harmonies and in enquiring into their meaning. He treats the same motif first in a warm colour scale, then in a cold scale; he juxtaposes his reds, pinks, yellows, greens, blues, purples with blacks and whites— and these too he raises to the level of colours. When painting women in an interior, one of his two favourite themes (the other is the still-life), Matisse often magnifies the figure until it almost fills the whole canvas, thus creating the striking immediacy of the cinema close-up. Elsewhere, on the other hand, he moves them away from us, plunging them into the atmosphere of their room, an atmosphere which has nothing hazy about it; its colours are sometimes vivid, sometimes muted, but never indecisive. As a rule the distance which is thus suggested is not deep when physically explored by the eye, but thanks to the evocative power of the colours, it is limitless to our imagination. With all his strokes of daring, there is nothing wild about Matisse's art in his final phase. Although perhaps less immediately pleasing than during the 1920s, and certainly less suave, it is no less filled with rich harmonies. Its salient features are accuracy, poise, proportion: in short, classicism. It is as foreign to convulsions of form as to those of the soul. There is no hypertension, no anguish, no terror, no wrinkle on the women's faces to show that they have experienced cares or sufferings. Very rarely, their gaze seems to betray some inner longing; but in general they express, not impassivity, but a profound peace and an indefinable, aloof tranquillity of mind. Their role in these works is scarcely different from that of the fruit or flowers, for Matisse's aim is never to worry or upset us, but rather to charm us (using the word with all its primary force here), to transport us to another world, created by him, where our souls find fresh strength as in gardens full of the most heady delights. 'Luxury, calm and delight'—*Luxe, Calme et Volupté*—the title of one of his earliest major compositions, might be borne by most of his paintings, particularly those painted after 1935 *(Pl. 205)*.

During the last years of his life, Matisse specialized in *papiers découpés* (paper cutouts); he cut out forms from pieces of paper which he had previously coloured over, thus achieving the closest and apparently the most natural union between colour and draughts-

205 Matisse STILL-LIFE WITH ETRUSCAN VASE 1940

manship. Each colour has an absolute purity, each is presented in the sharpest possible manner, whilst at the same time seeming almost disembodied—one might almost say retaining only the spirit of colour. No outlines define the different tones, which are placed side by side with the utmost freedom. The forms, for their part, are precise without being stressed; they are defined, and at the same time flowing; they are fixed, and yet one has the impression of seeing them take shape before our eyes. If as a rule the line has a nimble movement, it also experiences brief moments of hesitation, when it breaks off its course and turns sharply back on itself before setting off again with renewed vigour. It seems to be eternally oscillating between dexterity and clumsiness, but it is always incisive, remaining vibrant even when stiff. The forms can display complexities of curves and counter-curves, but the range of colours is often limited; some of these works use only a blue on a white ground. However, even when the palette is rich, as in *Zulma* of 1950 (Statens Museum for Kunst, Copenhagen) or *Sadness of the King* of 1952

206 Matisse SADNESS OF THE KING 1952

(Pl. 206) the whole is never lacking in clarity. On the contrary, the most extreme economy produces the greatest intensity. These *papiers découpés* are distinguished by a further trait: their monumental quality. They are well suited to the considerable dimensions which the artist often chose to give them; *Sadness of the King* measures 2.92 × 3.86 m., and this is not the biggest work of the series. And they have a true mural or, if one prefers it, decorative character, in the finest meaning of the term. Matisse also used the paper cutout technique to make designs for ceramics and stained glass windows. One of these last, *Christmas Eve* (1951) has been transported in glass to New York where it decorates the building of *Life* magazine.

Dufy, it will be remembered, had been guided towards fauvism by Matisse's example. Did this same example urge him to remain an advocate of pure colour? Possibly. What is certain is that pure colour was profoundly in tune with his temperament. It is true that he did draw away from it for a time. Painting side by side with Braque at L'Estaque in 1908, he practised an austere style of painting in which all forms were geometrized and, as it were, petrified, where the palette was restricted to ochres, blues, greens and greys—pre-cubism in fact. But Dufy did not remain for long an exponent of this manner. After doing work dyeing and painting on materials for the dress designer Paul Poiret and the Lyons silk manufacturer Bianchini, he returned to more vivid tonalities more in keeping with his optimistic temperament. Periods of time spent in Vence (1920–1), Sicily (1921) and Morocco (1921) helped him to discover and develop a style which is no less personal than that of Matisse.

The beaches and ports which attracted him in his fauve period continued to provide him with subjects. Now, however, he no longer restricted his choice to Normandy, choosing to visit the Riviera where the luminous blue of the sky and the Mediterranean fascinated him to such an extent that in *The Casino at Nice* of 1927 (Georges Moos collection, Geneva) he spread it over the Promenade des Anglais. On the other hand, in about 1923 he began to paint race-courses and paddocks, visiting Longchamp and Deauville, Ascot and Epsom, and expressing with wit and verve the animation, the high spirits, the elegance and the entertainment he found there. He was also inspired by music: a violin, a grand piano in *Homage to Mozart (Pl. 207)* provide him with enough material for a dense and concentrated work; but most often he likes to depict orchestras in a concert hall. Sometimes he confines his study to the musicians, striving to give colour equivalents of the varying sonorities which they draw forth from their instruments *(The Double-bass Players, Pl. 202),* sometimes showing, in addition to the orchestra, the solemn surroundings of the concert hall and the audience which is moved and enraptured by the music. Dufy also sometimes paints work on the land, the harvesting or threshing of corn; although not insensitive to the oppressive summer heat and the noisy jolting of the threshing machine, he pays less attention to the laborious aspect of the work than to the summery atmosphere and the pleasure derived from it. 'And even so,' he says, 'try as I might, I can only give you a tiny scrap of the joy in my heart.' No one has ever put more jubilation into the blue of a sky, more pleasure into that of the sea, more freshness and fragrance into the green of a meadow. Nor has any painter put more exhilaration, and at the same time more wit, into the purples and reds of a historic occasion. Indeed, in 1937, Dufy succeeded in painting *The Coronation of King George VI (Pl. 208)* with its huge flags, the royal procession, the double ranks of uniformed men, and the landmarks of London, without becoming either bombastic or trite.

Dufy constantly reveals his study of nature, without ever restricting himself to a mere imitation. One has the impression that he loves nature too much not to embellish it with all the attractions with which the poetic imagination can adorn it. Thus his colour enjoys a freedom limited neither by considerations of realism nor by those of draughtsmanship. It covers his canvases in blocks or dots, spilling over from the forms or only half-filling them. Supremely dextrous strokes, which suggest rather than depict objects, are superimposed on fields of colour so that the draughtsmanship remains intact no less than the colour, and each remains independent of the other. The objects appear less as fixed entities than as caught,

207
Dufy
HOMAGE
TO MOZART
1952

208 Dufy THE CORONATION OF KING GEORGE VI 1937

quivering, in the instant when they were still seeking their final identity. Like Matisse, Dufy is concerned with spatial perspective; and one is bound to say that some of his solutions are no less daring and original than those of his elder colleague. With little concern for the reduced size which distance imposes on objects, he gives bigger proportions to two birds than to his figures, although the latter appear to be no further away from us. In other words, when he constructs his distance, he takes into account not what has an 'objective' existence, but what he feels, what impresses him. He confers on objects a dimension and weight which they have for his mind and soul.

During the last years of his life Dufy began to simplify his painting. He abandoned contrasts, replacing them with a single colour which completely dominates the painting, and on which he places other related tones, or grey and white. As in the case of Matisse the extreme

economy of the colouring is matched by its purity and brilliance
(*Yellow Console with Violin, Pl. 209*). Here again Dufy's supple,
quick and witty line, applied on top of the colour, plays a major
role. Dufy was also interested in black, using it to render the most
intense, dazzling light. On the other hand, he told Pierre Courthion:
'What I would like to do at the moment would be to take up the
problem of colour again, leaving out the rule of complementaries.
I would like to experiment with those tonal contrasts or harmonies
which tradition has taught us to reject.' Shortly afterwards death
stayed his hand; but Dufy's work remains one of the most appealing
of individual contributions to modern art: no other fauve painter
has endowed pure colour with a deeper enchantment.

Conclusion

From the impressionists onwards, painting has moved progressively further from the naturalism established by the Renaissance. Its aim in asserting its freedom with regard to the visible world has been to achieve an increasingly independent creation which relates solely to the artist's inner vision. One has only to recollect the pronounced anti-naturalistic tendencies of the fauves to judge the importance of their contribution to the new art. Although the fauves never severed their contact with nature, they used it simply as a source of inspiration and a 'dictionary'. In other words, they felt less compunction than their predecessors about altering it, and as we have seen, these alterations were not exclusively expressive in purpose; often the motive was a purely aesthetic one. Thus a good many fauve pictures must be seen as pure pictorial facts.

The principal debt which modern painting owes to fauvism lies in the rehabilitation and the emancipation of colour. In their glorification of colour, the fauves were renewing a tradition whose origins lie deep in the French (and indeed the European) culture of the Middle Ages, particularly in its illuminated manuscripts and stained glass. The fauves also have links with other cultures which attached primary importance to colour: the Byzantine and those aspects of Asiatic culture represented by Arab, Persian and Indian miniatures, the paintings of the T'ang dynasty and Japanese prints.

Although the years 1908 to 1914 witnessed the decline of fauve influence in favour of cubism, after the First World War fauve methods were followed by painters like Aujame, Cavaillès, Legueult and Limouse. But these artists came onto the scene in a period which set little store by daring innovation; they consequently confined themselves to using vivid colours while remaining faithful on the whole to a realistic conception of nature. It is characteristic that they referred themselves only to Matisse's work of the 1920s, the period in his career when his work produced the fewest innovations. On the other hand, the generation which came to the fore during or shortly after the Second World War took up the most revolutionary aspects of their predecessors' work. Hence the combination of pure colour and invented form which characterizes the works of Estève, Gischia, Lapicque, Pignon, Bazaine, Manessier and Singier. Certainly, these artists have not reverted to fauvism; they are quite aware that since then there have been the cubists as well as Klee and Kandinsky. But Matisse remains one of the artists they turn to the most willingly. Two of these painters, Estève and Lapicque, notwithstanding differences in their technique in other respects, have constantly sought after the purest brilliance of colour.

Fauvism lives again in a different form in the aggressive manner of Lanskoy, just as echoes of it are to be found in the vigorous and vibrant flat tints which Nicolas de Staël began to use in about 1952. One could quote other artists who have drawn near to fauvism in their fondness for a brilliant palette. This does not necessarily mean that they came under fauve influence; it is perfectly possible that they could have discovered pure colour independently. Nevertheless, in the majority of cases, they could not fail to be encouraged by the fauve example. There is certainly no doubt that the leader of the fauve movement continues to act as advisor and guide from beyond the grave. Picasso himself, talking to Daniel-Henry Kahnweiler about the importance of colour in his variations on Delacroix's *Women of Algiers,* said: 'I sometimes think that this is the legacy of Matisse.'

Biographies

BRAQUE Georges. Born at Argenteuil on 13 May 1882. In 1890, his family settled in Le Havre where he went to the *lycée* and where he attended evening classes at the Ecole Municipale des Beaux-Arts. As it was intended that he should go into his father's house-painting business, he worked in Le Havre before going to Paris in 1900 to continue his apprenticeship. In 1901-2 he did a year's military service before returning to Paris, this time in order to go to an art school. He spent two years at the Académie Humbert in Montmartre and two months in Bonnat's studio at the Ecole des Beaux-Arts. After being influenced by impressionism, he joined the fauvists in 1906 and exhibited for the first time at the Salon des Indépendants. Together with Friesz, he painted in Antwerp (1906) and at La Ciotat (1907). He spent the autumn of 1906 at L'Estaque. Towards the end of 1907, he began to draw away from fauvism in order to create a more austere art in which construction played a greater role. In 1908, he worked in this new manner with Dufy at L'Estaque, showing his work at Kahnweiler's the same year. It was then that Louis Vauxcelles wrote in *Gil Blas:* 'M. Braque reduces everything... to cubes', a sentence which is the origin of the term 'cubism'. In 1909, Braque painted at La Roche-Guyon near Mantes, and in 1910 at L'Estaque once more. Meanwhile he and Picasso had become friends and until 1914 the two artists, living in close harmony, made parallel experiments together. They were together at Céret in 1911 and at Sorgues in 1912. They passed at the same time (1912) from analytical to synthetic cubism; they both did collages (1912-14). Braque returned to Sorgues in 1913. It was here that he received his mobilization papers. He was wounded and trephined in 1915 and invalided out of the army in 1917. When he returned to painting in Paris, the cubist group had dispersed, and from now on he evolved independently, whilst remaining faithful to certain cubist tenets. In 1919, he held a major exhibition at Léonce Rosenberg's gallery in Paris. In 1920, he executed his first piece of sculpture. In 1917 he had resumed the habit of spending his summers at Sorgues, but in 1929 he went to stay at Varengeville near Dieppe, where he later had a house built. During the 1930s some of his works were translated into tapestry form by Mme Cuttoli.

In 1937 he was awarded the Carnegie Prize. In 1939, he took up sculpture again. The German invasion in 1940 caused him to make for the Pyrenees, but he returned to Paris in the autumn. In 1948 he published some aphorisms and drawings under the title *Cahier de Georges Braque (1917-47)*. A supplement *(1947-55)* was added to this *Cahier* in 1956. The year 1948 brought him the First Prize at the Venice Biennale. In 1952-3 he designed a ceiling for the Etruscan room at the Louvre, and in 1953-4 he made designs for the stained-glass windows in a chapel at Varengeville.

Braque illustrated: Pierre Reverdy's *Les Ardoises du toit,* 1918; Erik Satie's *Le Piège de Méduse,* 1921; Diaghilev's *Les Fâcheux,* 1924; *Milarepa,* a Tibetan magician–poet, 1951; Pierre Reverdy's *Une Aventure méthodique,* 1953; Hesiod's *Theogony,* 1954. He designed scenery and costumes for the Ballets Russes *(Les Fâcheux,* 1923-4; *Zéphyr et Flore,* 1924-5), and for the Ballets du Comte de Beaumont *(La Salade,* 1925) as well as for Louis Jouvet (Molière's *Tartuffe,* 1950).

Bibliography: S. Fumet: *Braque,* Paris 1945; F. Ponge: *Braque,* Geneva 1946; J. Paulhan: *Braque le patron,* Geneva 1947; D. Cooper: *Braque,* London 1948; H.R. Hope: *Braque,* New York 1949; A. Lejard: *G. Braque,* Paris 1949; Jean Cassou: *Braque,* Paris 1956; M. Gieure: *Braque,* Paris 1956; F. Elgar: *Braque (1906-1920),* Paris 1958; A. Verdet: *Braque le solitaire,* Paris 1959; J. Richardson: *Georges Braque,* London 1959; J. Russell: *Georges Braque,* London 1959; J. Richardson: *Georges Braque,* Milan 1960; J. Leymarie: *Braque,* Geneva 1961.

C A M O I N Charles. Born in Marseilles on 23 September 1879. After taking drawing lessons in his native town, he went to Paris in 1896 and became a student in Gustave Moreau's studio at the Ecole des Beaux-Arts, where he met Matisse, Manguin and Rouault and made friends with Marquet, whose portrait he painted in 1904. About 1902 his military service took him to Aix-en-Provence, where he made the acquaintance of Cézanne. On his return to Paris in 1903, he began to exhibit at the Salon des Indépendants and at the Galerie Berthe Weill prior to taking part in the Salon d'Automne and the group exhibitions at the Galerie Druet. During

211
Vlaminck
PORTRAIT OF DERAIN

the winter of 1912-3 he accompanied Matisse and Marquet to Morocco, bringing back pictures showing Matisse's influence. During the 1914-18 war he enlisted in the camouflage section. In about 1916 he saw Renoir at Cagnes, and the effects of this meeting made themselves felt in his painting. In 1930 he and Marquet visited Spain. Having often stayed at Saint-Tropez between the Wars, he went back there in 1939 and did not return to Paris until 1944. He died there in 1965.

D E R A I N André. Born at Chatou on 10 June 1880. As his father wanted him to be an engineer, he prepared for entry to the Ecole Polytechnique but he preferred painting and from 1898 onwards he attended the Académie Carrière where he met Matisse. In 1900 he met Vlaminck, and the two painters rented a studio together near the bridge at Chatou. Derain had to do his military service from 1901 to 1903. 1905 was a particularly important year for him: Vollard came and bought up the whole of his studio; he made his first appearance at the Salon des Indépendants; during the summer at Collioure, side by side with Matisse, he painted fauve landscapes which he sent to the Salon d'Automne; finally, he went to London to work. He went back there again in the spring of 1906 and the same year he held an exhibition at the Galerie Berthe Weill. During 1907 he abandoned the fauve manner and began to move towards an art which allied austere colouring to a stylized and more rigid form. At the same time, he carried out his first pieces of sculpture and signed a contract with the cubists' dealer, Daniel-Henry Kahnweiler. In 1908, he left Chatou and settled in Montmartre. He made ceramics which were fired by Méthey. In 1910, he worked at Cadaquès (Spain) side by side with Picasso. His 'Gothic' period began in 1912 and lasted until 1914. The year 1913 saw him at Martigues with Vlaminck; 1914 with Picasso at Avignon. Called up for military service at the outbreak of war, he spent four years at the front. After the Armistice he reverted to realism, taking as his model the 'proven' art of the museums, painting landscapes (in the Lot department, in Italy, at St Maximin, Var, and elsewhere) as well as still-lifes, portraits and numerous nude studies. He was awarded the Carnegie Prize in 1928 and held a large-scale exhibition at Paul Guillaume's in 1931, his first in Paris since 1916. In 1935, he retired to Chambourcy (Seine-et-Oise).

He died in Paris in 1963.

He illustrated numerous books, notably Vlaminck: *D'un lit dans l'autre*, 1902 and *Tout pour ça*, 1903; Apollinaire: *L'Enchanteur pourrissant*, 1909; Max Jacob: *Les Œuvres burlesques et mystiques de Frère Martorel, mort au couvent*, 1912; André Salmon: *Le Calumet*, 1922; Vincent Muselli: *Les Travaux et les jeux*, 1929; Petronius: *Satyricon*, 1934; Ovid: *Heroides*, 1938; Rabelais: *Pantagruel*, 1946; La Fontaine: *Contes et Nouvelles*, 1950 and *Odes Anacréontiques*, 1955. He also designed scenery and costumes *(La Boutique fantasque* for the Ballets Russes, 1919; *Songes* for Balanchine's *Ballets 1933* ; *Que le diable l'emporte* for Roland Petit, 1948; *The Seraglio* and *The Barber of Seville* for the Aix-en-Provence Festival, 1951 and 1953.

Bibliography: Daniel-Henry (Kahnweiler): *André Derain*, Leipzig 1920; Elie Faure: *A. Derain*, Paris 1923; A. Salmon: *André Derain*, Paris 1929; A. Basler: *Derain*, Paris 1931; J. Leymarie: *André Derain, ou le retour à l'ontologie*, Geneva 1948; A. Derain; *Lettres à Vlaminck*, Paris 1955; M. Sandoz: *Eloge de Derain*, Paris 1959; G. Hilaire: *Derain*, Geneva 1959; Denys Sutton: *André Derain*, London 1960.

D U F Y Raoul. Born at Le Havre on 3 June 1877. From 1892 he attended evening classes at the Ecole Municipale des Beaux-Arts in his native town. Since Friesz attended the same classes, the two young painters became friends. They met again in Paris, in Bonnat's studio at the Ecole des Beaux-Arts, which Dufy entered in 1900. A year later he exhibited at the Salon des Artistes Français. He took part in the Salon des Indépendants for the first time in 1903 and in the Salon d'Automne in 1906, holding his first private exhibition at the Galerie Berthe Weill the same year. In the meantime he abandoned impressionism for fauvism. He painted in the fauve manner with Friesz at Falaise and with Marquet at Sainte-Adresse, Le Havre and Trouville (1906). Working side by side with Braque at L'Estaque in 1908, he temporarily abandoned fauvism in favour of an austere art of geometrical forms. In 1909 he visited Munich in the company of Friesz. The following year he met dress designer Paul Poiret, for whom he created textile designs with wood blocks which he himself had carved and with colours which he himself had mixed. In 1912 the Lyons silk manufacturer Bianchini engaged Dufy to work for him too. In 1917-18 Dufy was attached to the Musée de la Guerre, concerned with drawings and paintings.

In 1920-1 he lived for several months at Vence. From this time on his style progressively acquired a more personal character. In 1922, he passed through Florence and Rome on his way to stay in Sicily. The following year, he decorated ceramics made by Artigas and began to paint *Paddocks* and *Horse Races*. In 1925 he made a trip to Morocco accompanied by Poiret. The same year, at the Exposition Internationale des Arts Décoratifs, he exhibited a series of fourteen printed tapestries in Poiret's stands. In 1927 he painted at Nice; in 1928 in the Bois de Boulogne; in 1929-30 at Deauville. In 1932 he did tapestry cartoons for salon furnishings made by the Manufacture de Beauvais. At the Paris Exhibition in 1937 he carried out a vast composition (ten metres high and sixty metres long) for the Palais de l'Electricité, in which he retraced the history of electricity through the ages. This period marks the beginning of the arthritis from which he was to suffer for the rest of his life. In 1938 he visited Venice and Pittsburgh in the United States, where he served on the jury for the Carnegie Prize. In 1940, fleeing from the German invasion, he settled first of all in Nice, then Céret, then finally in Perpignan, where he did two cartoons for Aubusson tapestries. In 1942, he painted mostly *Orchestras* and *Studio Interiors ;* and in 1943 *Threshing Scenes.* Two years later he visited Spain, settling in Paris on his return. In 1950 he went to Boston to undergo a course of cortisone treatment, returning to France in 1951 after a stay in Tucson, Arizona. In 1952, the year in which he received the first Prize at the Venice Biennale, he settled near Forcalquier, where he died on 23 March 1953.

Dufy illustrated notably Apollinaire: *Le Bestiaire*, 1911; Mallarmé: *Madrigaux,* 1920; Fernand Fleuret: *Friperies,* 1924; Gustave Coquiot: *La Terre frottée d'ail,* 1925; Eugène Montfort: *La belle Enfant ou l'Amour à quarante ans,* 1930; Brillat-Savarin: *Aphorismes et Variétés,* 1940. He designed the scenery and costumes for *Palm Beach* (Ballets du Comte de Beaumont, 1926), Armand Salacrou's *Les Fiancés du Havre* (Comédie Française, 1944), *Ring around the Moon* (Jean Anouilh's *L'Invitation au Château,* Gilbert Miller, Boston, 1950).
Bibliography: Berr du Turique: *Raoul Dufy,* Paris 1930; P. Camo: *Dufy,* Lausanne 1946; J. Cassou: *Raoul Dufy,* Geneva 1946; Claude Roger-Marx: *Raoul Dufy,* Paris 1950; P. Courthion: *Raoul Dufy,* Geneva 1951; G. Besson: *Dufy,* Paris 1953; J. Lassaigne: *Dufy,* Geneva 1954; R. Cogniat: *Dufy,* Paris.

F R I E S Z Emile-Othon. Born at Le Havre on 6 February 1879. Like Dufy, he attended evening classes from 1892 onwards at the Ecole Municipale des Beaux-Arts in his native town. In 1898 he went to Paris where he entered the Ecole des Beaux-Arts as a pupil of Bonnat. In 1900 he exhibited at the Salon des Artistes Français. After his meeting with Pissarro and Guillaumin in 1901, he began to paint in the impressionist manner. He was represented at the Salon des Indépendants from 1903 and at the Salon d'Automne from 1904. Sometime during this period he began to exhibit at Druet's. His contacts with Matisse and other young artists encouraged his evolution towards fauvism. In 1904 he painted at Cassis, in 1905 at La Ciotat, in 1906 at Falaise (with Dufy) and Antwerp (with Braque). The same year he signed a contract with the dealer Druet, to whom he made over his whole output until 1912. From 1907 to 1909 he worked with the ceramicist Méthey. In 1908 he abandoned fauvism, placing emphasis on the structure of the picture. In 1909, he visited Munich in company with Dufy, bringing back some solidly constructed snow landscapes. Other travels took him to Portugal (1911), Belgium (1912), Piedmont and Tuscany (1920), and the United States (1938). After the First World War his painting, while still retaining its baroque design, became progressively more realistic. He painted portraits, nudes, still–lifes, landscapes. Having won a Carnegie Prize in 1924, he became a member of the Carnegie Foundation jury in 1938. In 1935 he designed a Gobelins tapestry entitled *Peace*. He died in Paris on 10 January 1949, having lived a great deal of his life in Toulon since 1922.

He was one of the founders of the Salon des Tuileries, and taught at the Académie Moderne, before and after the First World War, and at the Académie Scandinave, where he numbered amongst his pupils Gruber, Tailleux and Tal Coat (*c.* 1929), and finally at La Grande Chaumière. He illustrated a selection of Ronsard's *Poèmes* (1934) and designed scenery and costumes for *La Lumière* (performed in Scandinavia by the Tournées Durec, 1919).
Bibliography: A. Salmon: *E.-O. Friesz,* Paris 1920; F. Fleuret, Ch. Vildrac, A. Salmon: *Friesz,* Paris 1928; R. Brielle: *Othon Friesz,* Paris 1930; M. Gauthier: *Othon Friesz,* Geneva 1957.

H E C K E L Erich. Born at Döbeln, Saxony, on 31 July 1883. From 1897 to 1904 he was at school in Chemnitz where in 1901 he met Schmidt-Rottluff. In 1904 he enrolled at the Technische Hochschule in Dresden as an architecture student. There he met Kirchner and Bleyl, and in 1905 the three friends, together with Schmidt-Rottluff, founded *Die Brücke,* to which Heckel belonged until 1913. He spent the summers from 1907 until 1910 at Moritzburg in Saxony or at Dangast in Oldenburg. In 1909 he visited Italy for the first time. In November 1911 he left Dresden and settled in Berlin. His palette, hitherto vivid, became dull, whilst his forms became geometrical, doubtless due to the influence of cubism and his contacts with Marc, Macke and Feininger. In 1912 he took part in the Cologne *Sonderbund* exhibition, decorating a part of the chapel. He was called up for military service in 1914 and spent the war in the German army hospital service in Belgium. He met Ensor and Beckman at Ostend. After the Armistice he returned to Berlin, where he lived until 1944 while continuing to spend his summers working in the country. His travels took him to different parts of Germany, as well as Switzerland, France, England, Denmark, Sweden and Italy. In 1936 the Nazis classified him amongst the 'degenerate' painters, forbade him to pursue his artistic activities, and confiscated from German museums more than seven hundred of his works, which were sold or destroyed. From 1940 to 1942 he lived for some time in Carinthia. After an air-raid had destroyed his Berlin studio in 1944 he turned his back for ever on the capital and settled at Hemmenhofen near Lake Constance. From 1949 to 1954 he taught at the Karlsruhe *Akademie*. Heckel also did sculpture and etchings.

Bibliography: Ludwig Thormaehlen: *Erich Heckel,* Leipzig 1931; P.O. Rave: *Erich Heckel,* Leipzig 1948; L. Thormaehlen: *E. Heckel,* Karlsruhe 1953.

J A W L E N S K Y Alexej von. Born in Torschok (in the province of Tver in Russia) on 13 March 1864. Starting out on a military career, he became an officer in Moscow in 1887. Two years later he had himself transferred to St Petersburg, where he attended classes at the art school. In 1896 he left the Army and went to Munich with the aim of continuing his studies. There he attended Anton Azbé's art school until 1899. During the summer of 1903, while on a trip to Normandy, he broke his journey in Paris; and he returned there in 1905 after a stay in Brittany. The same year he exhibited at the Salon d'Automne, where he met Matisse, going on to paint in Provence and on the Riviera. During the summer of 1908 he worked at Murnau in the company of Kandinsky, with whom he founded the *Neue Künstlervereinigung* of Munich in 1909. His art at this period was brilliant and sumptuous in colouring, individual in its harmonies, yet closely akin to that of the fauves. In 1912, Jawlensky took part in the Cologne *Sonderbund* and was shown in Berlin with the *Blaue Reiter* artists at an exhibition presented by Herwarth Walden at the *Der Sturm* gallery. He was also to be found at the Erster Deutscher Herbstsalon ('first German Salon d'Automne') organized by Walden in 1913. In this same year he began to concentrate more on form, which he simplified to the point of making it schematic, a trait which he was to emphasize from now on until illness prevented his hand from expressing his mind's

concern for discipline. Forced to leave Germany at the outbreak of war, he lived in Switzerland until 1921, when he settled in Wiesbaden. In 1924, together with Kandinsky, Klee and Feininger, Jawlensky formed the *Blaue Vier* ('blue four') group. Under the Hitler régime his art was declared 'degenerate', his works disappeared from German museums, and he was forbidden to exhibit in public. He died on 15 March 1951.
Bibliography: Clemens Weiler: *A. von Jawlensky,* Cologne 1959.

K A N D I N S K Y Wassily. Born in Moscow on 4 December 1866. Five years later his family settled in Odessa where he entered the high school in 1876. In 1886 he went to Moscow University to study law and political economy. During a trip to northern Russia in 1889 he visited the Hermitage in St Petersburg and was deeply impressed by Rembrandt. In an exhibition of French impressionists held in Moscow in 1895, he was struck by the freedom with which Monet's *The Stacks* were painted. The following year he decided to become a painter and went to Munich to study at Anton Azbé's art school, where he met Jawlensky. In 1900 he studied at Franz Stück's Academy. A year later he founded the *Phalanx* group over which he presided and which survived until 1904. In 1904 he visited Holland, Odessa and Tunisia, and in the following year he went to Odessa and Rapallo. He exhibited at the Paris Salon d'Automne of 1904, becoming a member of this salon in 1905. From June 1906 to June 1907 he lived at Sèvres (Seine-et-Oise). Having lived for brief periods in Switzerland and Berlin, he returned to Munich in 1908 and began to paint at Murnau in Bavaria. He drew nearer to Jawlensky and the fauves by his use of a brilliant palette, whilst at the same time tending more and more to turn away from the external world; and in 1910 he carried out his first abstract work. In the meantime he founded (1909) the *Neue Künstlervereinigung* of Munich, which he left in 1911 in order to form, together with Marc, Macke and several others, the *Blaue Reiter* group whose first exhibition was opened at the end of that year. He also took part in the collective show which took place in 1912 at the *Der Sturm* gallery. In 1913 he exhibited at the Deutscher Herbstsalon organized by Herwarth Walden. The outbreak of war in 1914 forced him to return to Russia. After the Revolution he held various official cultural posts in Moscow. In 1921, however, he returned to Germany. He was appointed to teach at the Bauhaus in Weimar in 1922 and followed it when it moved to Dessau in 1925. His art, which before 1914 had been marked by a romantic impetuosity which had calmed down on his return to Russia, contained henceforward only rigorously geometrical forms; but neither fantasy nor movement nor, latterly, opulence of colour were excluded. In 1924 Kandinsky founded with Jawlensky, Klee and Feininger the *Blaue Vier* group. When the Bauhaus, which had been transferred to Berlin in 1932, was closed on Hitler's coming to power, Kandinsky went to live at Neuilly-sur-Seine. In Paris, where his first individual exhibition had been held in 1929, he frequented Arp, Delaunay, Magnelli, Miró, Mondrian and Pevsner. In 1937 he visited Klee in Switzerland. The same year the Nazis confiscated almost sixty of his works from German museums. He died on 13 December 1944.

Kandinsky published: *Über das Geistige in der Kunst* illustrated with original woodcuts, Munich 1912; *Klänge,* prose poems illustrated with wood-engravings, Munich 1913; *Rückblicke,* Berlin 1913; *Punkt und Linie zu Fläche,* Munich 1926. In addition, engravings by Kandinsky appeared in *Der Blaue Reiter,* Munich 1912; *Kleine Welten,* Berlin 1922; René Char's *Le Marteau sans maître,* 1934; Tristan Tzara's *La Main passe,* 1935.

Bibliography: W. Grohmann; *Kandinsky,* Leipzig 1924; M. Bill: *Kandinsky,* Basle 1949; Ch. Estienne: *Kandinsky,* Paris 1950; W. Grohmann: *Kandinsky, Life and Work,* Cologne, New York, Paris, Milan, 1958; H. Read: *Kandinsky,* London 1959; G. Aust: *Kandinsky,* Berlin 1960; M. Brion: *Kandinsky,* Paris 1960; J. Cassou: *Kandinsky,* Paris 1960; P. Volboudt: *Kandinsky (1896–1921)* and *(1922–1944),* 2 vol., Paris 1963; J. Lassaigne: *Kandinsky,* Geneva 1964.

KIRCHNER Ernst-Ludwig. Born in Aschaffenburg on 6 May 1880. Having lived for two years in Perlen near Lucerne, he became a pupil at the Chemnitz *gymnasium* in 1889. In 1898, he visited Nuremberg, where he was profoundly impressed by Albrecht Dürer's art. Three years later he went to study architecture at the Technische Hochschule in Dresden. Shortly afterwards he began to paint and in 1903 interrupted his studies in order to spend two semesters at an art school run by W. Debschütz and H. Obrist in Munich. In 1904, he saw an exhibition of French neo-impressionists. He returned to Dresden that same year to resume his architectural studies, and discovered the wood carving from the Pellew Islands in the Ethnographisches Museum. During the summer of 1905, together with his fellow-students Bleyl, Heckel and Schmidt-Rottluff, he founded *Die Brücke,* of which he was the leader. During the summers of 1907 to 1910 he and his companions used to go into the countryside around Moritzburg (Saxony) in order to paint outdoor scenes. It is during these four years that his colouring has the greatest brilliancy. At the end of 1911, he left Dresden for Berlin, where he and Pechstein opened the MUIM Institute *(Moderner Unterricht im Malen,* 'modern teaching methods in painting'). From 1911 to 1914 he spent his summers on Fehmarn Island in the Baltic. In 1912 he took part in the large-scale exhibition of modern art organized by the Cologne *Sonderbund* and, together with Heckel he decorated the temporary chapel built in the grounds of the exhibition. The following year, he wrote the *Chronik der Brücke,* which remained unpublished as the other members of the group would not approve its text. The works which he carried out in Berlin before the First World War have a less brilliant colouring than those of his Dresden period and their forms are more geometrized. From 1914 to 1915 Kirchner served in the army at Halle an der Saale, but he had to be invalided out and went into a sanatorium in Königstein (Taunus), where he decorated the stairwell with paintings inspired by his visits to Fehmarn. In 1917 he went to Switzerland, first to Davos, then to Kreuzlingen on Lake Constance. He finally settled in Frauenkirchen in 1918, where his art became more colourful. From 1929 to 1932 he did designs for murals for the Museum Folkwang in Essen, but Hitler's rise to power prevented him from carrying them out. In 1937 more than six hundred of his works were confiscated from German museums, and thirty-six of them appeared in the Nazi-organized exhibition of 'degenerate' art. Deeply wounded by the treatment meted out to him in his own country and broken in health, he committed suicide on 15 June 1938. In addition to his paintings, Kirchner did sculptures and numerous etchings.

Between 1910 and 1937 he published, sometimes under the pseudonym L. de Marsalle, various texts which appeared in exhibition catalogues or journals. He illustrated several works, in particular Chemisso's *Peter Schlemihl* (1916) and Georg Heym's *Umbra Vitae* (1924).

Bibliography: W. Grohmann: *Kirchner, Zeichnungen,* Dresden 1925; W. Grohmann: *Das Werk E.L. Kirchners,* Munich 1926; Gustav Schiefler: *Die Graphik E.L. Kirchners,* 2 vol., Berlin 1926 and 1931; Hans Fehr: *Erinnerungen an E.L. Kirchner,* Berne 1955; W. Grohmann: *E.L. Kirchner,* Stuttgart and London 1958; Annemarie Dube-Heynig: *E.L. Kirchner, Graphik,* Munich 1961.

M A C K E August. Born at Meschede on 3 January 1887. In 1900 his family settled in Bonn, where he was to spend much of his life. From 1904 to 1906 he studied art in Düsseldorf. He visited Italy in 1905 and 1908, and in 1907 and 1908 Paris, where he discovered the impressionists, Cézanne and Seurat, paying a further visit there in 1909. Towards the end of the same year he settled at Tegernsee in Bavaria, where he worked for a year. At the beginning of 1910 he and Franz Marc became friends. During the same period he went to an exhibition of Matisse's work in Munich. Macke professed deep admiration for Matisse, an admiration which is reflected in Macke's art. In 1911 he met Kandinsky and took part in the first exhibition of *Der Blaue Reiter.* In 1912 he was represented at the big *Sonderbund* exhibition in Cologne. The same year he returned to Paris accompanied by Marc and the two artists went to see Delaunay. From that moment on Matisse's influence waned, and cubism helped Macke to produce his most personal paintings. In 1914 he visited Tunisia with Klee and Moilliet. Shortly afterwards war broke out, Macke was called up and he was killed in action in Champagne on 16 September 1914.

Bibliography: Kurt Martin: *August Macke, Reise nach Kairouan,* Baden-Baden 1954; M.T. Engels: *August Macke,* Cologne 1956; W. Holzhausen: *August Macke,* Munich 1956; Gustav Vriesen: *August Macke,* Stuttgart 1953/1957; Wolfgang Macke: *August Macke, Aquarelle,* Munich 1958.

M A N G U I N Henri-Charles. Born in Paris on 23 March 1874. He entered Gustave Moreau's studio at the Ecole des Beaux-Arts in 1896, and there became a friend of Matisse, Marquet and Camoin. Like other future fauves, he met Pissarro and was influenced by

Cézanne and Gauguin. He exhibited at the Salon d'Automne from 1904, and at the Galerie Berthe Weill from 1903. During the fauve period he came under Matisse's influence, but never followed his friend's more daring experiments. In 1907 he visited Italy. He worked mostly in the south of France, especially at Saint-Tropez, where he died on 25 September 1949. He painted landscapes, nudes, still-lifes and portraits.

Bibliography: Pierre Cabanne: *Manguin,* Neuchâtel.

M A R C Franz. Born in Munich on 8 February 1880. At the age of twenty he became a student at the art academy of his native city, and remained there until 1903, when he went to Paris for several months. In 1905 he became mainly interested in animals as subjects and for three years he made numerous studies of them. In 1906 he went to Greece and visited Mount Athos. A further stay in Paris in 1907 brought Van Gogh and Gauguin to his notice, without however bringing about any changes in his style. In Munich, in 1909, he saw some of Jawlensky's and Kandinsky's brilliantly coloured works. The following year he met Kandinsky and Macke, whose current enthusiasm was Matisse: this period marks the point at which he adopted a vivid palette, giving a symbolic value to colours. In 1911 he joined the *Neue Künstlervereinigung* of Munich, which he left at the end of the year, at the same time as Kandinsky, with whom he founded *Der Blaue Reiter*. In 1912, he accompanied Macke to Paris, where he met the cubist Delaunay. Although he came under the influence of Delaunay and the Italian futurists, his works retained its romantic aura. He was represented at the Cologne *Sonderbund* exhibition in 1912 and in 1913 took part in the Erster Deutscher Herbstsalon in Berlin. The same year he began to evolve in the direction of abstract painting. His development was cut short by the outbreak of war; he enlisted at once and was killed at Verdun on 4 November 1916.

Bibliography: A.J. Schardt: *Franz Marc,* Berlin 1936; H. Demisch: *Franz Marc, der Maler des Neubeginns,* Berlin-Hanover 1948; Klaus Lankheit: *Franz Marc,* Berlin 1950; Georg Schmidt: *Franz Marc,* Berlin 1957; Max Robinson, *Franz Marc,* Paris 1963.

M A R I N O T Maurice. Born at Troyes in 1882. He came to Paris at the beginning of the century to study in Cormon's studio at the Ecole des Beaux-Arts. Guided by impressionist influences, by Gauguin and Cézanne as well as by what he saw at the Paris exhibitions, he painted, between 1905 and 1909, in a manner akin to that of the fauves, without having any personal contact with them. From 1904 to 1919 he exhibited regularly at the Salon des Indépendants and the Salon d'Automne. In about 1910 he returned to Troyes for good. In 1911 he learned how to make glass, a skill which he practised as long as his health allowed him to blow glass, that is to say until 1937. He died at Troyes in 1960.

M A R Q U E T Albert. Born in Bordeaux on 27 March 1875. After completing his secondary education there, he went to Paris in 1890, entering the Ecole des Arts Décoratifs, where he met Matisse. In 1895 he became a student at the Ecole des Beaux-Arts, where his teachers were Aimé Morot, Cormon and, after 1898, Gustave Moreau, in whose studio he met his friend Matisse again, remaining on close terms with him until his death. In order to earn their living they were both obliged to take on work in interior decorating and in 1900 they did enormous friezes of laurel leaves at the Grand Palais. Although Marquet was using pure tones around 1898, he soon began to prefer muted tones, more suited to his

213
Marquet
SELF-PORTRAIT

temperament. He exhibited at the Salon des Indépendants from
1901, at the Salon d'Automne from 1903, at the Galerie Berthe Weill
from 1902 and at the Galerie Druet from 1904. In 1905 he signed
a contract with Druet, and in 1907 he held his first one-man exhibition there. He was essentially a landscape painter delighting in
painting the Paris *quais* as well as doing ports and beaches. From
1904 to 1932 he worked at Fécamp, Le Havre, Sainte-Adresse,
Naples, Hamburg, Conflans, Collioure, Rouen, Tangiers, Rotterdam, Marseilles, Algiers, Bordeaux, Stockholm and elsewhere. In
1940 he settled in Algiers for the duration of the war. He returned
to Paris in 1945 and visited the USSR in 1946. He died in Paris on
14 June 1947.

Books illustrated by Marquet include Eugène Montfort: *Mon
brigadier Triboulère,* 1918; Marcelle Marty: *Moussa, le petit noir* 1925,
etc.

Bibliography: Marquet: *Dessins,* Le Point, Lanzac 1943; G. Besson:
Marquet, Paris 1947; G. Besson: *Marquet,* Geneva 1948; Marcelle
Marquet: *Marquet,* Paris 1952; M. Marquet and F. Daulte: *Marquet,*
Paris 1953; Marcelle Marquet: *Marquet,* Paris 1955; F. Jourdain:
Marquet, Paris.

M A T I S S E Henri. Born at Le Cateau-Cambrésis (Nord) on
31 December 1869. On the completion of his secondary education at Saint-Quentin he went to Paris to study law (1887-8),
after which he went to work as a clerk in a solicitor's office in Saint-
Quentin. The following year, while convalescing after an illness,
he began to paint. Although he started by taking a small treatise by
Goupil as his mentor, he subsequently attended art classes at the
Ecole Quentin-Latour. In 1892 he returned to Paris to attend an art
school. He enrolled for evening classes at the Ecole des Arts
Décoratifs, where he met and became friends with Marquet. He
also worked at the same time at the Académie Julian where his
teachers were William Bouguereau and Gabriel Ferrier. He failed
the entrance examination to the Ecole des Beaux-Arts, but in 1895
Gustave Moreau took him into his studio, without his having to
take an examination. In Moreau's studio he met Rouault, Evenepoel,
Flandrin, Camoin, Manguin, and others. Marquet joined him there
in 1898. In 1896 he made his début at the Salon de la Société Natio-
nale des Beaux-Arts and, in the company of the painter Emile Wéry,
made a visit to Brittany during the course of which John Russell,

a friend of Monet's, revealed to him the impressionists and Van Gogh. Some time later Pissarro taught him to admire Cézanne. In 1898-9 he lived for periods in Corsica and Toulouse. His palette, which had become clearer in Brittany, now became vivid and warm. When he returned to Paris, Cormon, who had been appointed professor in Gustave Moreau's place on the latter's death, asked him to leave the studio. He then (1899) went to the Académie Carrière, where he numbered among his fellow students Derain and Jean Puy. In order to keep his family he was obliged to undertake interior decorating work, including miles of laurel leaves in the Grand Palais, which was being got ready for the Exposition Universelle in 1900. But he already appears as leader of the little group of fauves drawn from amongst students from Gustave Moreau's studio and from the Académie Carrière. Aware of the importance of form and at the same time concerned with the properties of colour, he began in about 1900 to sculpt as well. He exhibited for the first time at the Salon des Indépendants in 1901, at the Salon d'Automne in 1903, at the Galerie Berthe Weill in 1902, at the Galerie Druet in 1904. It was also in 1904 that he gave his first private show at the Galerie Vollard. Whilst working that same year in Saint-Tropez, in the same neighbourhood as Signac, he began to use the divisionist technique. The following year, at Collioure, he abandoned this technique and painted the canvases to which, at the 1905 Salon d'Automne, the epithet 'fauve' was applied.

In 1906 he returned to Collioure after having stayed for a brief period at Biskra in Algeria. On his return to Paris he met Picasso. In 1907 he travelled in Italy. During the winter of 1907-8 he opened an academy in Paris where he taught until 1911 and where his pupils included Germans, Swedes, Norwegians, Americans, and Hungarians. In about 1907-8, he did some ceramics in collaboration with Méthey. In 1908 he visited Munich and Berlin. In 1909 he left Paris to settle at Issy-les-Moulineaux. A year later he went back to Munich, accompanied by Marquet and the German painter Hans Purrmann, who was a pupil of his, to see an exhibition of Islamic art there. He went to Spain early in 1911; in the autumn of that year, in response to an invitation from the collector Shchukin for whom he had painted two large-scale compositions, *The Dance* and *Music,* he set off for Moscow. Some weeks later he was in Morocco, where he spent the winter. The following winter he returned to Morocco in the company of Marquet and Camoin. In 1913 he took a studio in Paris again, whilst keeping on his house at Issy-les-Moulineaux. Having spent the winter of 1916–17 in Nice, he decided to return there and henceforward spent the greater part of his time on the Riviera. In 1917–18 he met Renoir at Cagnes. He also met Bonnard at Antibes. His painting had become progressively starker and more austere over the last few years; now it became more relaxed and immediately pleasing to the eye. From 1920 to 1930 he travelled little: he visited London in 1920, Etretat in 1920 and 1921 and Italy in 1925, but he worked above all in Nice and Paris. He was awarded the Carnegie Prize in 1927. He sailed to the United States on being chosen three years later as a member of the jury for this Prize. During this same year he made a visit to Tahiti which he was later to exploit in designing tapestry cartoons *(Window in Tahiti,* 1935; *Polynesia: Sea and Sky,* 1946. In 1930 Dr Barnes of Merion commisioned him to do a large mural *(La Danse)* which was finished in 1933. It was while carrying out this work, which ushered in a new period of fauvism for him, that Matisse used for the first time the *papiers découpés* (paper cutouts) which became a major interest towards the end of his life. In 1938 he settled at Cimiez, and in 1943 at Vence. In 1947 he began to work out the details of plans for the design and decoration of a chapel for the Dominican nuns of Vence, which was finished in 1951. In the meantime (1949) he returned to Cimiez, where he died on 3 November 1954.

Matisse wrote a book entitled *Jazz* (text and *papiers découpés,* 1947) and illustrated several others, in particular Pierre Reverdy: *Les Jockeys camouflés,* 1918; Mallarmé: *Poésies,* 1932; Montherlant: *Pasiphaé,* 1944; *Les Lettres portugaises,* 1946; Baudelaire: *Les Fleurs du Mal,* 1947; Ronsard: *Florilège des Amours* 1948; Charles d'Orléans: *Poèmes,* 1950. In addition he designed scenery and costumes for *L'Étrange Farandole* (Ballets de Monte-Carlo, 1938).

Bibliography: M. Sembat: *H. Matisse,* Paris 1920; J. Guenne: *Portraits d'artistes,* Paris 1927; F. Fels: *H. Matisse,* Paris 1929; Courthion: *Matisse,* Paris 1934; R. Escholier: *Matisse,* Paris 1937; J. Cassou: *Matisse,* Paris 1939; P. Courthion: *Le Visage de Matisse,* Lausanne 1943; A. Lejard: *Matisse,* Paris 1943; G. Besson: *Matisse,* Paris 1943; Aragon: *Matisse,* Geneva 1946; A. Lejard: *Matisse,* Paris 1948;

A.H. Barr Jr: *Matisse,* New York 1951; A. Verdet: *Prestiges de Matisse,* Paris 1952; G. Diehl: *Matisse,* Paris 1954; G. Duthuit: *Matisse (période fauve),* Paris 1956; J. Lassaigne: *Matisse,* Geneva 1959; J.-L. Ferrier: *Matisse (1911-1930),* Paris 1961; Jean Selz: *Matisse,* Paris.

M O D E R S O H N - B E C K E R Paula. Born Paula Becker in Dresden on 8 February 1876. Between 1892 and 1896 she studied in London, Bremen and Berlin. In 1897 she worked at Worpswede near Bremen. She settled there a year later and in 1901 she married the painter Otto Modersohn, who was living there. She had in the meantime been to Paris to study at the Académie Colarossi and the Ecole des Beaux-Arts (1900). Greatly impressed by Cézanne, she returned to Paris in 1903, 1905 and 1906. During this last visit she saw the Gauguin exhibition at the Salon d'Automne, and it was he who now exercised a decisive influence on her. She returned to Worpswede in 1907 and died on 21 November of the same year. *Bibliography:* Gustav Pauli: *Paula Modersohn-Becker,* Berlin 1919; G. Biermann: *Paula Modersohn-Becker,* Leipzig 1927; R. Hetsch: *Paula Modersohn-Becker, ein Buch der Freundschaft,* Berlin 1932; M. Hausmann: *Paula Modersohn-Becker,* Biberach/Riss 1947.

N O L D E Emil. Born Emil Hansen at Nolde in northern Schleswig on 7 August 1867. In 1884 he started to train to be a woodcarver in Flensburg, and he worked later as a woodcarver in furniture factories in Munich and Karlsruhe. It was in the latter town that he attended classes in 1899. Towards the end of this year he got a job as a furniture designer in Berlin. From 1892 to 1898 he taught design at the Gewerbeschule in St Gall. In 1894, he began to paint and to have postcard reproductions made of his watercolours in which the Swiss Alps resemble the faces of fantastic giants. Two years later he did his first painting. In 1898 he set up in Munich, and, as he failed to gain admission to the Academie, he enrolled at a private school, prior to going to work with Adolf Hölzl in Dachau in 1899, spending several months of that year in Paris, where he studied at the Académie Julian. In 1903, having lived in Copenhagen and Berlin, he settled on the island of Alsen in Denmark, where he spent much of his time during the following years, and where he was joined in 1907 by Schmidt-Rottluff, who shortly before had applied to Nolde for admission to *Die Brücke*. Nolde was a member of this association until 1907 and took part in the exhibitions which it organized in Dresden (1907) and also in Hamburg and Flensburg (1908). It was some while later that he evolved the expressionist style to which he remained faithful for the rest of his life. During the course of a trip he made in 1911 to Belgium and Holland he met Ensor and was struck with admiration for Rembrandt and Franz Hals. The following year he bought Utenwarf, a house near Ruttebüll (Schleswig) where, until 1926, he liked to spend his summers, whilst most frequently following an already established habit of spending his winters in Berlin. A group of nine paintings devoted to the life of Christ which he did in 1912, and which were to have been shown at the Exposition Universelle in Brussels, were rejected, following Church intervention. The same year he was represented at the second exhibition of *Der Blaue Reiter* in Munich and at the *Sonderbund* exhibition in Cologne. In 1913 the German Colonial Office invited him to undertake a journey to New Guinea in the course of which he travelled through Russia, Korea, Japan and China. In 1921 he visited France and Spain and, in 1925, Italy. Two years later he went to live at Seebüll (Schleswig), whilst continuing for some time to keep up his habit of spending his winters in Berlin. Although he had been an early member of the National Socialist Party, his art was judged 'degenerate' by the Nazis, and in 1937 more than a thousand of his works were confiscated. In 1941 he was, in addition, forbidden to pursue his artistic activities. The following year his Berlin studio was destroyed in an air raid. In 1950 he was awarded the prize for his etchings at the Venice Biennale. He died on 13 April 1956.

Nolde published various works of autobiography: *Das eigene Leben,* Berlin 1931, Flensburg 1949; *Jahre der Kämpfe,* Berlin 1934, Flensburg 1957; *Welt und Heimat,* 1912–1918; *Reisen, Ächtung, Befreiung,* 1919–1946.

Bibliography: Max Sauerlandt: *Emil Nolde,* Munich 1921; Paul-Ferdinand Schmidt: *Emil Nolde,* Leipzig 1929; Fritz Baumgart: *Emil Nolde, ein Gedenkbüchlein,* Rudolstadt 1946; Hans Fehr: *Emil Nolde, ein Buch der Freundschaft,* Cologne 1957; M. Gosebruch: *Nolde, Aquarelle und Zeichnungen,* Munich 1957; Günther Busch:

Nolde, Aquarelle, Munich 1957; Werner Haftmann: *Emil Nolde,* Cologne 1958.

PECHSTEIN Max. Born in Zwickau on 31 December 1881. From 1900 to 1902 he studied at the school of decorative arts and at the Akademie in Dresden. In 1906 he joined the *Brücke.* The following year he went on a journey to Italy and to Paris, where he saw fauve works and met Van Dongen. In 1908 he settled in Berlin. Having been turned out of *Die Brücke* in 1912 he visited the Pellew Islands in 1913-14. After the war, in which he served on the western front, he settled in Berlin where he remained until the Nazis banned him from exhibiting his paintings. He then retired to Pomerania. In 1945 he returned to Berlin and was given a teaching post. He died there on 20 June 1955.
Bibliography: G. Biermann: *Max Pechstein,* Leipzig 1919; M. Osborn: *Max Pechstein,* Berlin 1922; Konrad Lemmer: *Max Pechstein und der Beginn des Expressionismus,* Berlin 1949.

PURRMANN Hans. Born in Speyer on 10 May 1880. After studying in Karlsruhe and Munich, he went to Paris in 1906, where he became one of Matisse's principal pupils at his academy. Later, he drew nearer to Renoir without forgetting the teaching of his former master. He lived in Berlin from 1916 to 1935, whilst spending his summers either in Italy or near Lake Constance. He left Germany in 1935 and settled in Florence, after his art had been declared 'degenerate' by the Nazis. He has been living at Montagnola in the Ticino since the end of the last war.
Bibliography: Erhard Göpel: *Leben und Meinung des Malers Purrmann,* Baden-Baden.

PUY Jean. Born in Roanne on 8 November 1876. He studied at the Ecole des Beaux-Arts in Lyons (1895-8) and the Académie Julian (1898) and the Académie Carrière in Paris (1899). It was there that he met Matisse, under whose influence he turned towards Cézanne and became a representative of moderate fauvism. In 1901 he began to exhibit at the Salon des Indépendants, in 1904 at the Salon d'Automne and in 1903 at the Galerie Berthe Weill. He painted in Brittany, at Belle Isle and Concarneau, in the Roanne region, at

Collioure, and elsewhere. But he was not only a landscape artist; he painted numerous nudes, children, interiors and flower pieces. He died at Roanne in 1960. He illustrated Ambroise Vollard's *Le Père Ubu à la guerre* (1923).

Bibliography: P. Gay: *Jean Puy,* Paris 1944.

S C H M I D T - R O T T L U F F Karl. Born Karl Schmidt at Rottluff near Chemnitz on 1 December 1884. He attended the Chemnitz *gymnasium,* where he met Heckel in 1901. Four years later he went to the Technische Hochschule in Dresden where he made the acquaintance of Kirchner and Bleyl and, together with them and Heckel, founded *Die Brücke.* In 1906 he made contact with Nolde and worked side by side with him at Alsen (Denmark). From 1907 to 1914 he stayed on several occasions at Dangast near the North Sea. He spent the summer of 1911 painting in Norway. His colouring, always rich and vibrant, now became more intense. At the end of the year he, like his colleagues, set up in Berlin where he came into contact with Otto Müller and Feininger. Henceforward his palette lost its vivacity, and his form revealed the influence of cubism and Negro sculpture. From 1915 to 1918 he served with the army on the Russian front. After the war he went back to Berlin. He travelled in Italy, Dalmatia and Holland, visited Paris and stayed in the Ticino (1928-9) and in Rome (1930). In 1937 the Nazis classified him among the 'degenerate' painters, and confiscated more than six hundred of his works. In 1941 he was forbidden to continue painting. In 1947 he became a teacher of art in Berlin. Schmidt-Rottluff has also done sculpture and wood-engravings.

Bibliography: W.R. Valentiner: *Schmidt-Rottluff,* Leipzig 1920; Rosa Schapire: *Schmidt-Rottluffs graphisches Werk,* Berlin 1924; W. Grohmann: *Karl Schmidt-Rottluff,* Stuttgart 1956.

S M I T H Matthew. Born in Halifax, Yorkshire, on 22 October 1879. He studied at the Manchester School of Art and at the Slade School in London. He went to France in 1908 and worked at Pont-Aven, Dieppe and Etaples before settling in Paris in 1910, where he became a student at Matisse's academy. This was closed shortly afterwards, so Smith saw very little of the master. He was nonetheless deeply influenced by Matisse and Gauguin, and he

never lost his love of pure tones. After his return to England in 1912 he spent two further periods in France (1912, 1913-14), during which he evinced a great admiration for Ingres. In 1914 he settled in London; six years later he retired to Cornwall. In 1923 he was back in Paris again and lived chiefly in France until 1938. After Paris and Dieppe it was the south of France that attracted him during the thirties: Arles, Cagnes and finally Aix-en-Provence, where he settled for a few years. During the winter of 1938-9 he returned to London. After the Second World War he rediscovered France and discovered Venice (1958), but most of his time was spent in England. He died in London on 29 September 1959.
Bibliography: Sir Philip Hendy, F. Halliday and J. Russell: *Matthew Smith,* London 1962.

V A L T A T Louis. Born in Dieppe on 8 August 1869. His studies at the Académie Julian put him in touch with the *nabis.* Later he exhibited with some of them on various occasions at Druet's. He made his début at the Salon des Indépendants at 1894. In 1896 he accompanied Maillol to Banyuls and helped him create his first sculptures. In 1905 Vollard, who had become his dealer in 1900 and who remained so until 1912, persuaded him to take up sculpture himself. At the 1905 Salon d'Automne his works were hung in the fauve room. Until the outbreak of war in 1914 he lived at Anthéor in the Esterel region, where he came into contact with Cross and Renoir. After 1914 he spent most of his time in Paris. He died in Paris on 2 January 1952.
Bibliography: R. Cogniat: *Louis Valtat,* Neuchâtel 1963.

V A N D O N G E N Kees. Born on 26 January 1877 at Delfshaven near Rotterdam. He enrolled first of all at a school of decorative arts with a view to becoming an industrial designer. But painting, with Van Gogh and the impressionists as his models, exercised a greater appeal for him. In 1897 he went to Paris. To keep himself in the beginning he took on all sorts of jobs: as a furniture remover, a porter at the *Halles,* a house-painter, doing portraits on the terraces of cafés. He also contributed drawings to satirical papers, *L'Assiette au beurre* in particular. Druet became interested in him in 1903; Vollard showed his work in 1904 and

Berthe Weill in 1905. In 1904 he made his début at the Salon des Indépendants and in 1905 at the Salon d'Automne. It was about this time that he went to live in Montmartre, in the *Bateau-Lavoir,* where he met Picasso. His fauve period lasted until about 1913. While going back to Holland from time to time over the years, he also visited Morocco, Tunisia, Spain, Egypt. Later, he painted at Deauville, on the Riviera, in Venice, that is to say, in the chosen haunts of high society. After the First World War he became the portrait painter of elegant women, actresses, people in the public eye (Anatole France, Boni de Castellane, and others). A naturalized Frenchman since 1929, he now lives in Monte-Carlo.

He has illustrated Dr J.C. Mardrus: *Hassan Badreddine-El Bass Raòui* (1925); Paul Leclère: *Venise seuil des eaux* (1925); Paul Poiret: *Deauville* (1931), etc. He has written: *Van Dongen raconte ici la vie de Rembrandt et parle à ce propos de Rembrandt, des femmes et de l'art,* Paris 1927.

Bibliography: Ed. des Courrières: *Van Dongen,* Paris 1925; P. Fierens: *Van Dongen,* Paris 1927.

V L A M I N C K Maurice de. Born in Paris on 4 April 1876. In 1879 his parents, who were musicians, settled at Le Vésinet. He learnt the violin, gave music lessons, and worked as an orchestral violinist. From about 1895 he was a professional racing cyclist for several years. He started to paint, taking advice from a member of the Société des Artistes Français, Robichon, and from a primitive painter who worked as a saddler in Le Vésinet. It was while he was living in Chatou that he met Derain in 1900 and up to the time when the latter was called up for military service (1901) the two young painters met regularly and worked together. In 1901, Vlaminck visited the Van Gogh exhibition at the Galerie Bernheim-Jeune in Paris. There he met Matisse and, inspired by Van Gogh's example, he shortly afterwards became the most expressionist and the most violent of the fauves. In 1905 he exhibited for the first time at the Salon des Indépendants and the Salon d'Automne. In 1906 he showed at the Galerie Berthe Weill. The same year Vollard bought up his whole studio. It was also during this period that he began to mix with the *Bateau-Lavoir* and Café Azon groups in Montmartre (including Picasso, Van Dongen, Max Jacob, Apollinaire, André

Salmon and Charles Dullin). In 1908 he abandoned fauvism in favour of a somewhat austere style influenced by Cézanne, and probably the cubists as well. In 1910 he held his first one-man show at the Galerie Vollard (with paintings and ceramics done by Méthey). In 1911 he visited London and Southampton. In 1913 he painted with Derain in Martigues and Marseilles. During the First World War he was an industrial draughtsman at the Loucheur factories in Suresnes and the air-station at Le Bourget. In 1919, seeking solitude, he left Paris and retired to Valmondois in the valley of the Oise. Five years later he settled at Rueil-la-Gadelière where he lived until his death in 1958. After 1920 his painting is expressionist and realist. In his landscapes as well as in his still-lifes and flowers, he sought dramatic effects of *chiaroscuro*.

Vlaminck composed cartoons for tapestries as well as theatre scenery (for *Un Homme marche* by Henri Marx, produced by Tournées Durec, 1919). He illustrated Vanderpyl: *Voyages* (1920); Gabriel Reuillard: *Grasse Normandie* (1926); R. Radiguet: *Le Diable au corps* (1926); Georges Duhamel: *Les Hommes abandonnés* (1927), etc. He also wrote several books of his own, notably *D'un lit dans l'autre,* illustrated by Derain, Paris 1902; *Tout pour ça,* illustrated by Derain, Paris 1903; *Communications,* poems, Paris 1920; *Tournant dangereux,*

Paris 1929; *Poliment,* Paris 1931; *Désobéir,* Paris 1936; *Portraits avant décès,* Paris 1943.

Bibliography: Florent Fels: *Vlaminck,* Paris 1928; K.G. Perls: *Vlaminck,* New York 1941; P. Mac-Orlan: *Vlaminck,* Paris 1947; M. Genevoix: *Vlaminck,* Paris 1954; M. Sauvage: *Vlaminck, sa vie et son message,* Geneva 1956; J.P. Crespelle: *Vlaminck, fauve de la peinture,* Paris 1958; Jean Selz: *Vlaminck,* Paris; Pierre Cabanne: *Vlaminck (Paysages),* Paris 1966.

W O U T E R S Rik. Born in Malines, Belgium, on 21 August 1882. In 1902 he became a sculpture student at the Académie des Beaux-Arts in Brussels. A year later he began to paint. On leaving art school he lived successively in Watermael, Malines and Brussels, before finally settling in Boitsfort near Brussels. All his life he enjoyed painting and sculpting, but his major paintings began to appear only after 1912. It was in that year that visits to Paris and Cologne gave him his first chance of seeing original work by Cézanne, Renoir, Van Gogh and the impressionists. But he had already conceived a deep admiration and respect for Cézanne whom he knew in reproduction, just as he admired Ensor, whom he knew personally. He was mobilized in 1914, and after the fall of Antwerp he crossed into Holland where he was interned at Amersfoort. In 1915 he was released and settled in Amsterdam, where he died on 11 July 1916.

Bibliography: A.J.J. Delen: *Rik Wouters, zijn Leven, zijn werk, zijn einde,* Antwerp 1922; A.J.J. Delen: *Rik Wouters,* Antwerp 1922; Nel Wouters: *La Vie de Rik Wouters,* Brussels, 1944; Roger Avermaete: *Rik Wouters,* Brussels 1962.

Select General Bibliography

Gaston Diehl: *Les Fauves,* Paris 1943; Georges Duthuit: *Les Fauves,* Geneva 1949; G. Marussi: *I "Fauves",* Venice 1950; Joseph-Emile Muller: *Le Fauvisme,* Paris 1956; Jean Leymarie: *Le Fauvisme,* Geneva 1959; Gotthard Jedlicka: *Der Fauvismus,* Zurich 1961; J.P. Crespelle: *Les Fauves,* Neuchâtel 1962; Charles Chassé: *Les Fauves et leur temps,* Lausanne 1963.

List of the Plates

The medium is oil on canvas unless stated otherwise.

1 Matisse *Nude* 1906. Lithograph. Museum of Modern Art, New York.

2 Matisse *Fiacre* 1900. Brush drawing. Musée du Cateau.

3 Marquet *Fiacre c.* 1900. Brush drawing. Private collection, Paris.

4 Page from *L'Illustration*, 4 November 1905, reproducing paintings by Manguin, Matisse (*Pls. 21, 22*), Derain, Puy and Valtat exhibited at the Salon d'Automne.

5 Matisse Study for *The Joy of Living* 1905. Ink drawing.

6 Matisse *Studio of Gustave Moreau* 1895. Private collection, Paris.

7 Matisse Copy of Raphael's *Baldassare Castiglione c.* 1894. Musée de Bagnols-sur-Cèze.

8 Matisse *Corsican Landscape* 1898. Musée des Beaux-Arts, Bordeaux.

9 Matisse *The Countryside around Toulouse* 1898-9. Georges Renand, collection, Paris.

10 Matisse *Still-life against the Light* 1899. Private collec., Pontoise.

11 Matisse *Interior with Harmonium* 1900. Musée Matisse, Nice.

12 Matisse *Nude with Pink Shoes* 1900. Daelmans collection, Brussels.

13 Matisse *Nude putting up Hair* 1901. National Gallery of Art, Washington.

14 Matisse *Carmelina* 1903. Museum of Fine Arts, Boston.

15 Matisse *Pont Saint-Michel* 1900. Private collection, Pontoise.

16 Matisse *Notre-Dame* 1902. Private collection, Paris.

17 Matisse *View of Saint-Tropez* 1904. Musée de Bagnols-sur-Cèze.

18 Matisse Study for *Marquet painting a Nude* 1904-5. Musée National d'Art Moderne, Paris.

19 Matisse *Pastoral* 1905. Musée du Petit Palais, Paris.

20 Matisse *Olive Trees* 1905. Lehman collection, New York.

21 Matisse *Woman with Hat* 1905. Walter A. Haas collection, San Francisco.

22 Matisse *Open Window, Collioure* 1905. Mr and Mrs John Hay Whitney collection, New York.

23 Matisse Study for *The Joy of Living* 1905. Statens Museum for Kunst, Copenhagen.

24 Matisse *The Joy of Living* 1905-6. Barnes Foundation, Merion, Pennsylvania.

25 Matisse *Luxe, calme et volupté* 1904-5. Mr and Mrs John Hay Whitney, New York.

26 Matisse Study for *Luxe, calme et volupté* 1904. Mr and Mrs John Hay Whitney collection, New York.

27 Matisse *The Gipsy* 1905-6. Musée de l'Annonciade, Saint-Tropez.

28 Matisse *Nude* 1906. Wood-engraving. Museum of Modern Art, New York.

29 Matisse *Seated Nude* 1906. Lithograph.

30 Matisse *Margot* 1907. Kunsthaus, Zurich.

31 Matisse *Still-life with Red Carpet* 1906. Musée des Beaux-Arts, Grenoble.

32 Matisse *Marguerite reading* 1906. Musée des Beaux-Arts, Grenoble.

33 Matisse *The Siesta (Interior at Collioure)* 1905. Private collection, Ascona.

34 Matisse *Luxury I* 1907. Musée National d'Art Moderne, Paris.

35 Matisse *Luxury II* 1907-8. Statens Museum for Kunst, Copenhagen.

36 Matisse *The Young Sailor* 1906. Leigh B. Block collection, Chicago.

37 Matisse *Pink Onions* 1906. Statens Museum for Kunst, Copenhagen.

38 Matisse *The Bank* 1907. Kunstmuseum, Basle.

39 Matisse *Music* 1907. Museum of Modern Art, New York.

40 Matisse *Blue Nude – Souvenir of Biskra* 1907. Museum of Art, Baltimore.

41 Matisse *Boy with Butterfly Net* 1907. Institute of Arts, Minneapolis.

42 Vlaminck *Man with Red Scarf* 1900. Musée National d'Art Moderne, Paris.

43 Vlaminck *Little Girl with Doll* 1902. Private collection, Paris.

44 Vlaminck *Quai Sganzin at Nanterre* 1902. R. Varenne collection, Geneva.

45 Vlaminck *Pond at Saint-Cucufa c.* 1903. B.J. Fisz collection, Paris.

46 Vlaminck *Kitchen Interior* 1904. Musée National d'Art Moderne, Paris.

47 Vlaminck *Gardens at Chatou* 1904. Art Institute, Chicago.

48 Vlaminck *Road at Marly-le-Roi* 1905-6. Musée National d'Art Moderne, Paris.

49 Vlaminck *Barge* 1905. Bridgestone Museum, Tokyo.

50 Vlaminck *Village* 1906. Ragnar Moltzau collection, Oslo.

51 Vlaminck *The Bar Counter* 1900. Musée Calvet, Avignon.

52 Vlaminck *Picnic* 1905. Private collection, Paris.

53 Vlaminck *Dancer at the 'Rat Mort'* 1906. Fried collection, Paris.

54 Vlaminck *The Seine at Carrières-sur-Seine* 1906. Guy Roncey collection, Paris.

55 Vlaminck *Red Trees* 1906. Musée National d'Art Moderne, Paris.

56 Vlaminck *Bathers* 1907. Private collection, Paris.

57 Vlaminck *The Lock at Bougival* 1908. The National Gallery of Canada, Ottawa.

58 Vlaminck *Bateaux-Lavoirs* 1905. Private collection, Paris.

59 Vlaminck *Portrait of Derain* 1905. Private collection, Paris.

60 Derain *Ball at Suresnes* 1903. City Art Museum, Saint-Louis.

61 Derain *Trees c.* 1903. A. Kyrilis collection, Paris.

62 Derain *The Bridge at Le Pecq* 1904. Roger Gros collection, Paris.

63 Derain *Snow Landscape at Chatou* 1904-5. Private collection, Paris.

64 Derain *L'Age d'Or* 1905. Walter P. Chrysler, Jr. collection, New York.

65 Derain *Mountains at Collioure* 1905. Mr and Mrs John Hay Whitney collection, New York.

66 Derain *Côte d'Azur, near Agay* 1905-6. The National Gallery of Canada, Ottawa.

67 Derain *Portrait of Vlaminck* 1905. Mme Vlaminck collection, Rueil-la-Gadelière.

68 Derain *Barges* 1904. B.J. Fisz collection, Paris.

69 Derain *Self-Portrait* 1904. Mme Derain collection, Chambourcy.

70 Matisse *Portrait of Derain* 1905. Tate Gallery, London.

71 Matisse *Self-Portrait* 1906. Statens Museum for Kunst, Copenhagen.

72 Derain *Portrait of Matisse* 1905. Tate Gallery, London.

73 Derain *Sunset in London* 1905. Pierre Lévy collection, Troyes.

74 Derain *Bridge over the Thames* 1906. Musée de l'Annonciade, Saint-Tropez.

75 Derain *The Houses of Parliament* 1905. Musée de l'Annonciade, Saint-Tropez.

76 Monet *The Houses of Parliament* 1904. Musée de l'Impressionnisme, Paris.

77 Derain *London Bridge* 1906. Museum of Modern Art, New York.

78 Derain *Collioure* 1905. Pierre Lévy collection, Troyes.

79 Derain *Effects of Sun on Water* 1905. Musée de l'Annonciade, Saint-Tropez.

80 Derain *Woman in Chemise* 1906. Statens Museum for Kunst, Copenhagen.

81 Derain *Pool of London* 1906. Tate Gallery, London.

82 Derain *Vineyards in Spring* 1906. Kunstmuseum, Basle.

83 Marquet *Travelling Fair at Le Havre* 1906. Musée des Beaux-Arts, Bordeaux.

84 Marquet *Pont-Neuf* 1906. National Gallery of Art, Washington.

85 Marquet *Beach at Sainte-Adresse* 1906. B.J. Fisz collection, Paris.

86 Marquet *Fauve Nude* 1898. Musée des Beaux-Arts, Bordeaux.

87 Marquet *Portrait of Mme Matisse* 1901. Musée Masséna, Nice.

88 Marquet *Sergeant of the Colonial Army* 1907. Lehman collection, New York.

89 Camoin *Portrait of Marquet c.* 1905. Musée National d'Art Moderne, Paris.

90 Marquet *Portrait of André Rouveyre* 1904. Musée National d'Art Moderne, Paris.

91 Marquet *Sergeant of the Colonial Army* 1907. Musée des Beaux-Arts, Bordeaux.

92 Matisse *Marquet painting a Nude* 1904-5. Musée National d'Art Moderne, Paris.

93 Marquet *Matisse painting a Nude in Manguin's Studio* 1904-5. Musée National d'Art Moderne, Paris.

94 Marquet *Apse of Notre-Dame* 1902. Private collection, Paris.

95 Marquet *Quai des Grands-Augustins* 1905. Musée National d'Art Moderne, Paris.

96 Marquet *Beach at Fécamp* 1906. Musée National d'Art Moderne, Paris.

97 Marquet *Fourteenth July in Le Havre* 1906. Private collection, Paris.

98 Marquet *Sunset at Sainte-Adresse* 1906. M. Boulard collection, Créteil.

99 Marquet *Seated Nude*. Brush drawing.

100 Marquet *Happy Man*. Brush drawing.

101 Marquet *Woman doing her Hair*. Brush drawing.

102 Marquet *Woman with an Umbrella* 1901. Brush drawing.

103 Marquet *Man from behind* 1901. Brush drawing.

104 Marquet *Japanese Woman* 1901. Brush drawing.

105 Valtat *At Maxim's* 1895. Oscar Ghez collection, Geneva.

106 Valtat *Water Carriers at Arcachon* 1897. Oscar Ghez collection, Geneva.

107 Valtat *Promenade on the Champs-Élysées* 1898. Oscar Ghez collection, Geneva.

108 Manguin *Portrait of Jean Puy* 1906. Private collection, Paris.

109 Manguin *Seated Nude* 1903. Ink drawing.

110 Manguin *Fourteenth July at Saint-Tropez* 1905. Mme Manguin collection, Paris.

111 Valtat *Seine and Eiffel Tower* 1904. B.J. Fisz collection, Paris.

112 Dufy *Self-Portrait* 1898. Formerly Mme Dufy collection.

113 Dufy *Rigged Yacht* 1904. Nouveau Musée des Beaux-Arts, Le Havre.

114 Dufy *Window with Coloured Panes* 1906. Private collection, Paris.

115 Dufy *Old Houses at Honfleur* 1906. Dr Roudinesco collection, Paris.

116 Dufy *Sunshades* 1906. Dr Roudinesco collection, Paris.

117 Marquet *Hoardings at Trouville* 1906. Rottembourg-Roncey collection, Paris.

118 Dufy *Hoardings at Trouville* 1906. Musée National d'Art Moderne, Paris.

119 Dufy *Fourteenth July at Le Havre* 1906. Musée National d'Art Moderne, Paris.

120 Dufy *Le Havre Harbour c.* 1906. Von der Heydt Museum, Wuppertal.

121 Dufy *The Beach at Sainte-Adresse* 1906. Mr and Mrs John Hay Whitney collection, New York.

122 Dufy *Effects of Sun, Sainte-Adresse* 1906. Statens Museum for Kunst, Copenhagen.

123 Dufy *The Apéritif* 1908. Musée du Petit Palais, Paris.

124 Dufy *Anglers c.* 1908. Museum of Modern Art, New York.

125 Dufy *Jeanne with Flowers c.* 1907. Nouveau Musée des Beaux-Arts, Le Havre.

126 Dufy *Lady in Pink* 1907-8. Musée National d'Art Moderne, Paris.

127 Friesz *Portrait of Fernand Fleuret* 1907. Musée National d'Art Moderne, Paris.

128 Friesz *Harbour at Antwerp* 1906. Pierre Maurs collection, Paris.

129 Braque *Harbour at Antwerp* 1906. National Gallery of Canada, Ottawa.

130 Friesz *Landscape at La Ciotat* 1907. Pierre Lévy collection, Troyes.

131 Braque *The Landing-Stage, L'Estaque* 1906. Musée National d'Art Moderne, Paris.

132 Braque *L'Estaque* 1906. Aimé Maeght collection, France.

133 Braque *Harbour at Antwerp* 1906. Kunstmuseum, Basle.

134 Braque *House behind Trees* 1906. Lehman collection, New York.

135 Braque *La Ciotat* 1907. Pierre Lévy collection, Troyes.

136 Braque *La Ciotat* 1907. Musée National d'Art Moderne, Paris.

137 Braque *La Ciotat* 1907. Private collection, France.

138 Van Dongen *Women at a Balustrade* 1910. Musée de l'Annonciade, Saint-Tropez.

139 Van Dongen *Anita* 1905. Private collection, Monaco.

140 Van Dongen *The Sideshow* 1904–
5. Bernheim-Jeune collection,
Paris.

141 Van Dongen *Portrait of Kahnweiler* 1907. Oscar Ghez collection, Geneva.

142 Van Dongen *La Belle Fathma
and her Troupe* 1906. B.J. Fisz
collection, Paris.

143 Van Dongen *Old Clown c.* 1906.
Oscar Ghez collection, Geneva.

144 Van Dongen *Woman with Hat*
1908. Private collection, Paris.

145 Van Dongen *Liverpool Night
Club* 1906. Private collection,
Paris.

146 Van Dongen *Woman with Jewels*
1905. Max Moos collection,
Geneva.

147 Van Dongen *Portrait of Fernande Olivier* 1907-8. Oscar
Ghez collection, Geneva.

148 Van Dongen *Spanish Dancer c.*
1912. Musée National d'Art
Moderne, Paris.

149 Matisse *Seated Nude ; Foot* 1909.
Ink drawing. Art Institute,
Chicago.

150 Van Gogh *Portrait of the Artist
with Severed Ear* 1889. Leigh
B. Block collection, Chicago.

151 Matisse *Portrait with Green
Streak* 1905. Statens Museum
for Kunst, Copenhagen.

152 Derain *Three Figures in a Meadow* 1906. Musée du Petit Palais,
Paris.

153 Derain *Hyde Park* 1906. Pierre
Lévy collection, Troyes.

154 Gauguin *Vision after the Sermon*
1888. National Gallery of Scot-
land, Edinburgh.

155 Derain Wood-engraving for
Apollinaire's *L'enchanteur pourrissant* 1909.

156 Dufy *L'Estaque* 1908. Private
collection, Paris.

157 Braque *Houses at L'Estaque*
1908. Kunstmuseum, Berne.

158 Derain *Road to Beauvais* 1911.
Kunstmuseum, Berne.

159 Derain *Table by the Window c.*
1913. Pushkin Museum of Fine
Arts, Moscow.

160 Heckel *Two Men at a Table* 1913.
Wood-engraving.

161 Schmidt-Rottluff *Seated Woman*
1913. Wood-engraving.

162 Munch *The Cry* 1893. Wood-
engraving.

163 Kirchner *Young Girl with Blue
Divan* 1907-8. Institute of Arts,
Minneapolis.

164 Kirchner *Nude in Studio* 1910–
11. Staatliche Museen, Natio-
nalgalerie, Berlin.

165 Kirchner *Woman with naked
Torso, in a Hat* 1911. Wallraf-
Richartz-Museum, Cologne.

166 Kirchner *Dresden Street* 1907.
Private collection, Basle.

167 Kirchner *The Street* 1913. Museum of Modern Art, New
York.

168 Heckel *Nude on a Sofa* 1909.
Bayerische Staatsgemäldesamm-
lungen, Munich.

169 Heckel *Mill at Dangast* 1909.
Wilhelm-Lehmbruck-Museum,
Duisburg.

170 Heckel *Fasanenschlösschen (Hunting Lodge)* 1910. Wallraf-Ri-
chartz-Museum, Cologne.

171 Heckel *Brother and Sister* 1911.
Staatliche Kunsthalle, Karlsruhe.

172 Heckel *Two Men by a Table* 1912.
Kunsthalle, Hamburg.

173 Heckel *Harbour at Stralsund*
1912. Private collec., Stuttgart.